The Requisites of Enlightenment

Bodhipakkhiya Dīpanī

The Requisites of Enlightenment

Bodhipakkhiya Dīpanī

A Manual
by
the Venerable

Ledi Sayadaw

BPS Pariyatti Editions

BPS PARIYATTI EDITIONS
AN IMPRINT OF
PARIYATTI PUBLISHING
867 Larmon Road
Onalaska, WA 98570
www.pariyatti.org

Published with the consent of the original publisher.
Copies of this book for sale in the Americas only.

First BPS Pariyatti Edition: 2013

ISBN: 978-1-938754-37-1

Library of Congress Control Number: 2012920063

Printed in the USA

CONTENTS

Publisher's Foreword to the American Edition

In recent years, many people in the West have been exposed to the teachings of the Buddha through the practice of Vipassana meditation as taught by S.N. Goenka. Mr. Goenka was born in Burma (now Myanmar) where he learned this technique of meditation from Sayagyi U Ba Khin, who had in turn been taught by Saya Thetgyi. Saya Thetgyi had the fortune to learn Vipassana from the highly respected scholar and meditator monk Ledi Sayadaw.

In Burma, Ledi Sayadaw is well known, and in his lifetime was the author of more than 100 books that provided both clarification and inspiration regarding the teachings of the Buddha. As Vipassana meditation in the tradition of Ledi Sayadaw begins to spread in the West, we are fortunate to begin to gain broader access to his writings as well.

We are grateful to the Buddhist Publication Society of Sri Lanka for allowing us to co-publish The Requisites of Enlightenment. It is our sincere wish that this publication will prove valuable to those interested in understanding the Buddha's teaching at a deeper level, while providing the inspiration to continue walking step by step on the path.

Editor's Preface to the First Edition

With the present volume we present to our readers another treatise by the eminent Burmese scholar-monk, the late Venerable Ledi Sayadaw, whose life sketch appears in a work of his, published earlier in this series, A Manual of Insight *(Vipassanā Dīpanī).*[1]

We believe that this present treatise is one of the most helpful expositions of Dhamma which we have been privileged to publish in The Wheel series. It offers not only a wealth of information on many aspects of the Teaching, but is also a forcefully reasoned and stirring appeal to earnest endeavour towards the goal. We therefore wish to recommend this work to our readers' close and repeated study and reflection.

This treatise has been reproduced from the journal The Light of the Dhamma (Rangoon), which regrettably has ceased publication. For permission of reprint we are grateful to the publishers, The Union of Burma Buddha Sāsana Council, Rangoon.

In the present edition, many of the Pali terms used in the original have been supplemented or replaced by the English equivalents, for facilitating the reading of the treatise. The last chapter has been condensed. Otherwise only minor changes have been made in the diction.

In the original publication, the term *bodhipakkhiya-dhamma* had been rendered by "factors leading to enlightenment," which, however, resembles too closely the customary translation of the term *bojjhaṅga* by "factors of enlightenment" (see here Chapter VII). Therefore the title of the treatise in the original translation and the rendering of the term in the body of the text have been changed into "requisites of enlightenment", being one of the connotations of *bodhipakkhiya-dhamma*, as given in Chapter I. This nuance of meaning was chosen in view of the fact that this treatise does not deal with perfected constituents of enlightenment *(bodhi)* already achieved, but with the approach to that goal by earnest cultivation of

---

1 *The Wheel* No. 31/32

those seven groups of qualities and practices which form the thirty-seven *bodhipakkhiya-dhammas*.

A detailed table of contents and a comprehensive index have been added to this edition, for facilitating the use of this book.

Preface to the Second Edition

This edition is extensively indexed for study. Its index includes both Pali and English references. Moreover, a glossary has been added.

The Index refers to the English equivalents of the Pali words and phrases. The Glossary lists the words both in English and in Pali for easy reference. In some instances one English translation serves two Pali words; in others, the opposite occurs. Note is made when this occurs.

Translator's Preface

The Venerable Ledi Sayadaw's works are well-known in Burma. They are widely known because they are clear expositions of the Buddha Dhamma couched in language easily intelligible to an ordinary educated Burman. Yet, the Venerable Sayadaw's works are not meant for an absolute beginner of Buddhist studies. There are many Buddhist technical terms that require a certain amount of previous foundation in Buddhist tradition and practice.

The Venerable Sayadaw's exposition contains many technical Pali terms that are used by him as if they were ordinary Burmese words. Many of these terms have been incorporated into the Burmese language either in their original Pali form or with slight variations to accord with Burmese euphony. These are words that Burmans have made no attempt to translate, but have preferred to absorb them into the normal usage of the Burmese language. I have similarly made no attempt to translate many of them into English in the present translation. I have use these words in their original Pali form, though in all such cases an attempt has been made to append short explanatory footnotes in order to facilitate continuity in reading.

Though the translation is not verbatim, yet a careful attempt has been made to render as nearly a verbatim translation as in possible in the circumstances, having regard to differences in the construction of sentences between English and Burmese, to differences in the manner of presentation and to the Venerable Sayadaw's penchant for sometimes using extremely long sentences.

Many of the subheadings are not in the original text, but have been introduced by the translator for assisting the English reader.

The Venerable Sayadaw was a prolific writer. His works number over a hundred. Each of these works was written at the specific request of one or more of his numerous disciples, either as an answer to certain questions put to him, or, as in the present case, to expound certain important points or aspects of the Buddha-Dhamma.

Sein Nyo Tun
135, University Avenue,
Rangoon

Bodhipakkhiya-Dīpanī

Manual of the Requisites of Enlightenment

Introduction

In compliance with the request of the Pyinmana Myo-ok Maung Po Mya and Trader Maung Hla, during the month of Nayon, 1266 Burmese Era (June, 1904 C.E.), I shall state concisely the meaning and intent of the thirty-seven *Bodhipakkhiya-dhammas*, the requisites of enlightenment.

Four Types of Capacity for Path Attainment

It is stated in the *Puggalapaññatti* (the "Book of Classification of Individuals," (p. 160) and in the *Aṅguttara Nikāya* (AN 4:133) that, of the beings who encounter the *Sāsana*, i.e., the Teaching of the Buddha, four classes can be distinguished, viz.:

1. *Ugghāṭitaññu*
2. *Vipañcitaññu*
3. *Neyya*
4. *Padaparama*

Of these four classes of beings, an *ugghātiṭaññū* (one who understands immediately) is an individual who encounters a Buddha in person,[1] and who is capable of attaining the paths and the fruits through the mere hearing of a short concise discourse.

A *vipañcitaññū* is an individual who has not the capability of attaining the paths and the fruits through the mere hearing of a short discourse, but who yet is capable of attaining the paths and the fruits when the short discourse is expounded to him at some length.

A *neyya* is an individual who has not the capability of attaining the paths and the fruits through the hearing of a short discourse or when it is expounded do him at some length, but is one for whom it is

1 This is not mentioned in the canonical texts referred to above, and their commentaries. (Editor)

necessary to study and take careful note of the sermon and the exposition, and then to practice the provisions contained therein for days, months, and years, in order that he may attain the paths and the fruits.

This *neyya* class of individuals can again be subdivided into many other classes according to the period of practice which each individual finds necessary before he can attain the paths and the fruits, and which further is dependent on the *pāramīs* (perfections) which each of them has previously acquired, and the *kilesas* (defilements) which each has surmounted. These classes of individuals include on the one hand those for whom the necessary period of practice is seven days, and on the other, those for whom the necessary period of practice may extend to thirty or sixty years.

Further classes also arise, as for example in the case of individuals whose necessary period of practice is seven days; the stage of an *arahat* may be attained if effort is made in the first or second period of life,[2] while no more than the lower stages of the paths and the fruits can be attained if effort be made only in the third period of life.

Then, again, putting forth effort for seven days means exerting as much as is in one's power to do so. If the effort is not of the highest order, the period of necessary effort becomes lengthened according to the laxity of the effort, and seven days may become seven years or longer.

If the effort during this life is not sufficiently intense as to enable one to attain the paths and the fruits, then release from worldly ills cannot be obtained during the present Buddha Sāsana while release during future Buddha Sāsanas can be obtained only if the individual encounters them. No release can be obtained if no Buddha Sāsana is encountered. It is only in the case of individuals who have secured *niyata-vyākaraṇa* ("sure prediction" made by a Buddha), that an encounter with a Buddha Sāsana and release from worldly ills is certain. An individual who has not attained "sure prediction" cannot be certain either of encountering a Buddha Sāsana or achieving release from worldly ills, even though he has accumulated sufficient *pāramīs* to make both these achievements possible.

---

2 Three periods of life are usually distinguished, viz. youth, middle, and old age. See *Path of Purification* (*Visuddhimagga*), tr. by Bhikkhu Ñāṇamoli, p. 721.

These are considerations in respect of those individuals who possess the capabilities of attaining the paths and the fruits by putting forth effort for seven days, but who have not obtained "sure prediction."

Similar considerations apply to the cases of those individuals who have the potential to attain the paths and the fruits by putting forth effort for fifteen days, or for longer periods.

A *padaparama* is an individual who, though he encounters a Buddha Sāsana, and though he puts forth the utmost possible effort in both the study and practice of the Dhamma, cannot attain the paths and the fruits within this lifetime. All that he can do is to accumulate good habits and potentials (*vāsanā*).

Such a person cannot obtain release from worldly ills during this lifetime. If he dies while practising *samatha* (tranquillity) or *vipassanā* (insight) and attains rebirth either as a human being or a *deva* in his next existence, he can attain release from worldly ills in that existence within the present Buddha Sāsana.

Thus did the Buddha declare with respect to four classes of individuals.

Three Types of Patients

In the same sources referred to above, the Buddha gave another classification of beings, dividing them into three classes resembling three types of sick persons,[3] namely:

1. A person who is certain of regaining health in due time even though he does not take any medicine or treatment
2. A person who is certain of failing to make a recovery, and dying from the illness, no matter to what extent he may take medicines or treatment
3. A person who will recover if he takes the right medicine and treatment, but who will fail to recover and die if he fails to take the right medicine and treatment

3 Puggala-paññatti pp. 100f; AN 3:22 Aṅguttara Nikāya, Tika-nipāta (The Threes). No. 22 (see *The Wheel* No. 155–158, p.18).

Persons who obtained "sure prediction" from previous Buddhas, and who as such are certain of obtaining release from worldly ills in this life resemble the first class of sick persons.

A *padaparama* class of individual resembles the second class of sick persons. Just as this second class of sick person has no chance of recovery from his illness, a *padaparama* class of individual has no chance of obtaining release from worldly ills during this life. In future lives, however, he can obtain release either within the present Buddha Sāsana or within future Buddha Sāsanas. The story of the youth Chattamāṇava,[4] of the frog who became a *deva*,[5] and of the ascetic Saccaka[6] are illustrations of persons who obtained release from worldly ills in following existences within the present Buddha Sāsana.

A *neyya* class of individual resembles the third class of sick persons. Just as a person of this third class is related to the two ways of either recovering or dying from the sickness, so is a *neyya* individual related to the two eventualities of either obtaining release from worldly ills during the present life, or failing to obtain such release.

If such a *neyya* individual, knowing what is good for him according to his age, discards what should be discarded, searches for the right teacher, and obtains the right guidance from him and puts forth sufficient effort, he can obtain release from worldly ills in this very life. If, however, he becomes addicted to wrong views and wrong ways of conduct; if he finds himself unable to discard sensual pleasures; if although able to discard sensual pleasures he does not obtain the guidance of a good teacher; if he is unable to evoke sufficient effort; if although inclined to put forth effort he is unable to do so through old age; if although young he is liable to sickness; in all these cases he cannot obtain release from worldly ills in this present life. King Ajātasattu,[7] the millionaire Mahādhana's son,[8] bhikkhu Sudinna,[9] are cases of persons who could not obtain release from worldly ills in this present existence.

4 Vimānavatthu.
5 Vimānavatthu.
6 MN 36
7 Dīgha Nikāya 2: Sāmaññaphala Sutta.
8 Dhammapada Commentary and Petavatthu.
9 Vinaya Pitaka, Pārājika.

King Ajātasattu failed to obtain release because he had committed parricide. It is stated that he will drift in future *saṃsāra* (round of rebirths) for two *asaṅkeyyas* (unit followed by 140 zeros) of world-cycles, after which he will become a *paccekabuddha* (Solitary Buddha).

The millionaire Mahādhana's son indulged himself so excessively in sensual pleasures during his youth that he was unable to attain tranquillity of mind when he grew older. Far from obtaining release from worldly ills, he did not even get the opportunity of associating with the Tiratana.[10] Seeing his plight at that stage, the Buddha said to Ānanda: "Ānanda, if this millionaire's son had become a bhikkhu in my Sāsana during his youth or first period of his life, he would have become an *arahat* and would have attained Parinibbāna[11] in this present life. If, otherwise, he had become a bhikkhu during the second period of his life, he would have become an *anāgāmi*[12] and on death would have been reborn in the *suddhāvāsa-brahma-loka*,[13] whence he would attain Parinibbāna. In the next alternative, if he had become a bhikkhu in my Sāsana at the beginning of the third period of life, he would have become either a *sakadāgāmi* (once-returner) or a *sotāpanna* (stream-enterer) and would have attained permanent release from rebirth in the *apāya-lokas*."[14] Thus said the Buddha to the Venerable Ānanda. Thus, although he (the millionaire Mahādhana's son) possessed *pāramī* ripe enough to make his present life his last existence, not being a person who had secured "sure prediction," he failed to obtain release from worldly ills in his present life because of the upheavals caused by the defilements within him, and this is despite the fact that he had the opportunity of

10 *Tiratana*, "The Triple Gem": Buddha, Dhamma, Sangha.

11 "Full Nibbāna." The death of an *arahat* is known as attaining *parinibbāna*.

12 A non-returner, one who has attained the third of the four stages of sanctitude, who is no longer reborn in the world of sensuality (*kāma-loka*).

13 The Pure Abodes are a group of five heavens belonging to the form-sphere, where only the non-returners are reborn, and in which they attain arahatship and Nibbāna.

14 *Apāya-lokas*: The four lower worlds of misery. They are: the animal world, the ghost-world, the demon-world and hell.

encountering the Buddha Sāsana. If, further, his period of existence in the Lower Regions (*apāya-loka*) is prolonged because of evil acts done in this existence, he would not be able to rise again and emerge out of those *apāya-lokas* in time for the Sāsana of the future Metteyya Buddha. And, after that, the large number of world-cycles that follow are world-cycles where no Buddhas appear,[15] there being no world-cycles within the vicinity of the present world where Buddhas are due to appear. Alas! Far indeed is this millionaire's son from release from worldly ills even though he possessed *pāramī* ripe enough to make his present existence his last one.

The general opinion current at the present day is that if the *pāramīs* are complete, one cannot miss encountering a Buddha Sāsana even if one does not wish to do so, and that one's release from worldly ills is ensured even though one may not desire such release. Those of this view fail to pay attention to the existence of *niyata* (i.e., one who has obtained a sure prediction made by a Buddha) and *aniyata* (one who has not obtained a sure prediction made by a Buddha). Considering the two texts from the *Piṭakas* mentioned above, and the story of the millionaire Mahādhana's son it should be remembered that *aniyata-neyya* individuals can attain release from worldly ills in this life only if they put forth sufficient effort, even if they possess *pāramī* sufficient to enable them to obtain such release. If industry and effort are lacking, the paths and the fruits cannot be attained within the present Buddha Sāsana.

Apart from these classes of persons, there are also an infinite number of other beings who, like the ascetics Alāra and Uddaka (MN 28), possess sufficient *pāramī* for release from worldly ills, but who do not get the opportunity because they happen to be in one or the other of the eight inopportune places (*aṭṭhakkhaṇa*)[16] where it is not possible to attain the paths and the fruits.

---

15 *Suñña-kappas*: "Void" world-cycles.

16 DN 33.3.2, DN 34.2.1 p. 60; (1) *paccantaro*, a border district where the Buddha Sāsana does not flourish; (2) *arūpino*, the four brahma planes of the formless-sphere; (3) *vītaliṅgo*, persons with congenital defects such as idiocy, etc.; (4) *asaññasatta*, a brahma plane of the Form-Sphere of non-consciousness; (5) *micchādiṭṭhi*, birth among people holding wrong views; (6) *peta*, the Ghost world; (7) *tiracchāna*, the animal world; and (8) *niraya*, hell.

Necessary Conditions of Practice for *Neyya* and *Padaparama*

Of the four classes of individuals mentioned, the *ugghāṭitaññū* classes can attain the *sotāpattimagga* (path of a stream-enterer) and the other higher stages of wisdom—like Visākhā and Anāthapiṇḍika[17]—through the mere hearing of a discourse. It is not necessary for such individuals to practice the Dhamma according to the stages of purification, such as purification of virtue (*sīla-visuddhi*), of mind (*citta-visuddhi*) and so on. Be it remembered that this is also the case when *devas* and *brahmās* attain release from worldly ills.

Hence it should be noted that the courses of practice such as *sīla-visuddhi* and *citta-visuddhi*, laid down in the Pāli Canon, are only for the *neyya* and *padaparama* classes of individuals before their attainment of the *sotāpattimagga*. These courses of practice are also for the first three classes of individuals prior to the achievement of the higher stages of the paths and the fruits. In the period after the attainment of arahatship also, these courses of practice are used for the purpose of *diṭṭhadhamma-sukha-vihāra* (dwelling at ease in this present existence)[18], since Arahats have already gone through them.

After the passing of the first thousand years (of the present Buddha Sāsana), which constituted the times of the *paṭisaṃbhidhā-patta arahats* (Arahats possessing analytical knowledge), the period of the present Buddha Sāsana comprises the times of the *neyya* and *padaparama* classes of individuals alone. At the present day, only these two classes of individuals remain.

Neyya-puggala

Of these two classes of individuals, an individual of the *neyya* class can become a stream-enterer (*sotāpanna*) in this present life if he faithfully practices the *bodhipakkhiya-dhamma* comprising *satipaṭṭhāna* (four foundations of mindfulness), *sammāpadhāna* (right exertion), etc. If he is lax in his practice, he can become a

17 Dhammapada Commentary, stories relating to verses 1 and 18.

18 In an arahat there arises the knowledge of his freedom and he realizes: "Rebirth is no more; I have lived the pure life: I have done what ought to be done; I have nothing more to do for the realization of arahatship." Thus he lives at ease in this existence.

sotāpanna only in his next existence after being reborn in the *deva* planes. If he dies while still aloof from these (*bodhipakkhiya*) Dhammas, such as *satipaṭṭhāna*, etc., he will become a total loss so far as the present Buddha Sāsana is concerned, but he can still attain release from worldly ills if he encounters the Sāsana of the next Buddha.

Padaparama-puggala

An individual of the *padaparama* class can attain release within the present Buddha Sāsana after rebirth in the *deva* planes in his next existence, if he can faithfully practice these (*bodhipakkhiya*) Dhammas in his present existence.

The Age of *Ariyas* (Noble Ones) Still Extant

The five thousand years of the present Buddha Sāsana constitute, all of them, the age of saints. This age of saints will continue to exist so long as the Tipiṭakas (canonical scriptures) remain in the world. The *padaparama* class of individuals have to utilise the opportunity afforded by the encountering of the present Buddha Sāsana to accumulate as much of the nuclei or seeds of *pāramī* as they can within this lifetime. They have to accumulate the seeds of *sīla* (morality). They have to accumulate the seeds of *samādhi* (concentration). They have to accumulate the seeds of *paññā* (wisdom).

Morality (*Sīla*)

Of these three kinds of accumulations, *sīla*, *samādhi*, *paññā*, the seeds of *sīla* mean *pañca*-sīla,[19] *ājivaṭṭhamaka-sīla*,[20] *aṭṭhaṅga-uposatha-*

19 The five precepts. They are basic and constitute the minimum which every man or woman must observe. They are: abstention from killing, stealing, improper sexual intercourse, telling lies, and taking intoxicants.

20 The three constituents of the morality-group of the eightfold path when considered in detail, become *ājīvaṭṭhamaka-sīla* (morality ending with the practice of right livelihood) in the following way: (1) I will abstain from taking life, (2) I will abstain from stealing. (3) I will abstain from indulging in improper sexual intercourse and taking in-

sīla,[21] *dasaṅga-sīla*,[22] in respect of ordinary laymen and women, and the *bhikkhu-sīla*[23] in respect of the bhikkhus.

Concentration (*Samādhi*)

The seeds of *samādhi* mean the efforts to achieve *parikamma-samādhi* (preparatory concentration) through one or other of the forty subjects of meditation, such as the ten *kasiṇas* (meditation devices), or, if further efforts can be evoked, the efforts to achieve *upacāra-samādhi* (access concentration), or, if still further efforts can be evoked, the efforts to achieve *appanā-samādhi* (attainment concentration).

Wisdom (*Paññā*)

The seeds of *paññā* mean the cultivation of the ability to analyze the characteristics and qualities of *rūpa* (material phenomena), *nāma* (mental phenomena), *khandhā* (constituent groups of existence), *āyatana* (sense bases), *dhātu* (elements), *sacca* (truths), and the *paṭicca-samuppāda* (dependent origination), as well as the cultivation of insight into the three characteristics of existence (*lakkhaṇa*), namely, *anicca* (impermanence), *dukkha* (suffering), and *anattā* (impersonality).

---

toxicating drugs. (4) I will abstain from telling lies. (5) I will abstain from setting one person against another. (6) I will abstain from using rude and rough words. (7) I will abstain from frivolous talk. (8) I will abstain from improper livelihood.

21 The eight uposatha precepts are: abstention from (1) killing, (2) stealing, (3) unchastity, (4) lying, (5) intoxicants, (6) eating after midday, (7) dancing, singing, music and shows, garlands, scents, cosmetics and adornment, etc, and (8) luxurious and high beds.

22 The ten precepts. This is the polished form of *aṭṭha-sīla*. No. seven of the eight precepts is split into two parts, and no. 10 is "abstinence from accepting gold and silver."

23 *Bhikkhu-sīla*: the four kinds of the monk's moral purity (*catupārisuddhi-sīla*) are: (1) restraint with regard to the 227 Pātimokkha training rules, (2) restraint of the senses, (3) restraint with regard to one's livelihood, and (4) morality with regard to the four requisites.

Of the three kinds of seeds of path-knowledge (*magga-ñāṇa*) and fruition-knowledge (*phala-ñāṇa*),[24] *sīla* and *samādhi* are like ornaments that permanently adorn the world and exist even in the *suñña kappas*, that is, world-cycles where no Buddhas arise. The seeds of *sīla* and *samādhi* can be obtained at will at any time. But the seeds of *paññā*, which are related to *rūpa*, *nāma*, *khandhā*, *āyatana*, *dhātu*, *sacca*, and *paṭicca-samuppāda* can be obtained only when one encounters a Buddha Sāsana. Outside of a Buddha Sāsana one does not get the opportunity of even hearing the mere mention of words associated with *paññā*, though an infinite number of void world-cycles may have passed away. Hence, those persons of the present day who are fortunate enough to be born into this world while a Buddha Sāsana flourishes, if they intend to accumulate the seeds of path and fruition-knowledge for the purpose of securing release from worldly ills in a future existence within a future Buddha Sāsana, should pay special attention to the knowledge of the *paramattha*[25] (ultimate realities)—which is extremely difficult for one to come across—rather than attempting the accumulation of the seeds of *sīla* and *samādhi*. At the least, they should attempt to obtain an insight into how the four great primaries (*mahā-bhūtā*)—*paṭhavī*, *āpo*, *tejo*, and *vāyo*[26]—constitute one's body. If they acquire a good insight into the four great elements, they obtain a sound collection of the seeds of *paññā* which are most difficult of acquisition, and this is so even though they may not acquire any knowledge of the other portions of the Abhidhamma. It can then be said that the difficult attainment of rebirth within a Buddha Sāsana has been made worthwhile.

24 *Magga-ñāṇa*: knowledge of the four noble paths, i.e., of stream-entry, etc. *Phala-ñāṇa*: knowledge of the fruits thereof. *Paramattha* or Truth.

25 The *Abhidhammatthasaṅgaha* lists four *paramattha-dhammas*, namely, *citta* (consciousness/mind), *cetasika* (mental factors), *rūpa* (material qualities) and *nibbāna*.

26 *Paṭhavī* (element of extension), *āpo* (element of liquidity or cohesion), *tejo* (element of kinetic energy), and *vāyo* (element of motion or support); popularly called: earth, water, fire, and wind.

Knowledge (*Vijjā*), and Conduct (*Caraṇa*)

Sīla and *samādhi* constitute *caraṇa* (conduct) while *paññā* constitutes *vijjā* (knowledge). Thus are *vijjā-caraṇa* (knowledge-and-conduct) constituted. *Vijjā* resembles the eyes of a human being, while *caraṇa* resembles the limbs. *Vijjā* is like the eyes of a bird, while *caraṇa* is like its wings. A person who is endowed with morality and concentration, but lacks wisdom, is like one who possesses complete and whole limbs but is blind in both eyes. A person who is endowed with *vijjā* but lacks *caraṇa* is like one who has good eyesight but is defective in his limbs. A person who is endowed with both *vijjā* and *caraṇa* is like a normal whole person possessing both good eyesight and healthy limbs. A person who lacks both *vijjā* and *caraṇa* is like one defective in eyes and limbs, and is not worthy of being called a human being.

Consequences of Having *Caraṇa* Only

Amongst the persons living within the present Buddha Sāsana, there are some who are fully endowed with morality and concentration, but do not possess the seeds of *vijjā* such as insight into the nature of material qualities, mental qualities and constituent groups of existence. Because they are strong in *caraṇa* they are likely to encounter the next Buddha Sāsana, but because they lack the seeds of *vijjā* they cannot attain Enlightenment, even though they hear a discourse of the next Buddha in person. They are like Lāludāyi Thera,[27] Upananda Thera,[28] the Chabbaggīya bhikkhus,[29] and the King of Kosala[30] who all lived during the lifetime of the Omniscient Buddha. Because they were endowed with the previously accumulated good conduct such as generosity and morality, they had the opportunity to associate with the Supreme Buddha, but since they lacked previously accumulated knowledge the discourses of the Buddha which they often heard throughout their lives, fell, as it were, on deaf ears.

27 Dhammapada Commentary, story relating to Verse 64.

28 Dhammapada Commentary, story relating to Verse 158 "The Greedy Monk."

29 Vinaya Piṭaka, Mahāvagga.

30 Dhammapada Commentary, story relating to Verse 60.

Consequences of Having *Vijjā* Only

There are others who are endowed with *vijjā* such as insight into the material and the mental qualities and the constituent groups of existence, but who lack *caraṇa* such as *dāna* (generosity), *nicca sīla* (constant morality) and *uposatha-sīla* (precepts observed on Uposatha days). Should these persons get the opportunity of meeting and hearing the discourses of the next Buddha they can attain enlightenment because they possess *vijjā*, but since they lack *caraṇa* it would be extremely difficult for them to get the opportunity of meeting the next Buddha. This is so because there is an *antara-kappa* (intervening world-cycle) between the present Buddha Sāsana and the next.

In those cases where these beings wander within the sensuous sphere during this period, it means a succession of an infinite number of existences and rebirths; in these cases an opportunity to meet the next Buddha can be secured only if all these rebirths are confined to the happy course of existence. If, in the interim, a rebirth occurs in one of the four lower regions, the opportunity to meet the next Buddha would be irretrievably lost, for one rebirth in one of the four lower worlds is often followed by an infinite number of further rebirths in one or other of them.

Those persons whose acts of *dāna* (generosity) in this life are few, who are ill-guarded in their bodily acts, unrestrained in their speech, and unclean in their thoughts, and who thus are deficient in *caraṇa*, possess a strong tendency to be reborn in the four lower worlds when they die. If through some good fortune they manage to be reborn in the happy course of existence, wherever they may be reborn they are, because of their previous lack of *caraṇa* such as *dāna*, likely to be deficient in riches, and likely to meet with hardships, trials, and tribulations in their means of livelihood, and thus encounter tendencies to rebirth in the *apāya-lokas*. Because of their lack of the *caraṇa* of *nicca-sīla*, and *uposatha-sīla*, they are likely to meet with disputes, quarrels, anger and hatred in their dealings with other persons, in addition to being susceptible to diseases and ailments, and thus encounter tendencies towards rebirth in the *apāya-lokas*. Thus will they encounter painful experiences in every existence, gathering undesirable tendencies, leading to the curtailment of their period of existence in the happy course of existence and causing rebirth in the four lower worlds. In this way, the chances of those who lack *caraṇa* for meeting the next Buddha are very slight indeed.

The Essential Point

In short, the essential fact is, only when one is endowed with the seeds of both *vijjā* and *caraṇa* can one obtain release from worldly ills in one's next existence. If one possesses the seeds of *vijjā* alone, and lacks the seeds of *caraṇa* such as *dāna* and *sīla*, one will fail to secure the opportunity of meeting the next Buddha Sāsana. If, on the other hand, one possesses the seeds of *caraṇa* but lacks the seeds of *vijjā*, one cannot attain release from worldly ills even though one encounters the next Buddha Sāsana. Hence, those *padaparama* individuals of today, be they men or women, who look forward to meeting the next Buddha Sāsana, should attempt to accumulate within the present Buddha Sāsana the seeds of *caraṇa* by the practice of *dāna*, *sīla* and *samatha-bhāvanā* (practice of tranquillity meditation), and should also, at the least, with respect to *vijjā*, try to practice insight into the four great primaries and thus ensure meeting the next Buddha Sāsana, and having met it, to attain release from worldly ills.

When it is said that *dāna* is *caraṇa*, it comes under the category of *saddhā*, which is one of the *saddhammas* or practical attributes of good people, which again comes under the fifteen *caraṇa-dhammas*. The fifteen *caraṇa-dhammas* are:

1. *Sīla* (morality)
2. *Indriya-saṃvara* (guarding the sense doors)
3. *Bhojane mattaññutā* (moderation in eating)
4. *Jāgariyānuyoga* (wakefulness)

5-11. *Saddhamma* (the seven attributes of good and virtuous people)

12-15. Four *jhānas* (meditative absorptions)

These fifteen *dhammas* are the property of the highest *jhāna-lābhi* (attainer of *jhānas*). So far as *sukkhavipassaka* (practising insight only) individuals are concerned, they should possess eleven of the *caraṇa-dhammas*, i.e., without the four *jhānas*.

For those persons who look forward to meeting the next Buddha Sāsana, *dāna*, *uposatha-sīla*, and the seven *saddhammas* are the essentials.

Those persons who wish to attain the paths and the fruits thereof in this very life must fulfil the first eleven *caraṇa-dhammas*, i.e., *sīla*, *indriya-saṃvara*, *bhojane mattaññutā*, *jāgariyānuyoga*, and the seven *saddhammas*. Herein, *sīla* means *ājīvaṭṭhamaka-nicca-sīla* (permanent practice of morality ending with right livelihood) and *indriya-saṃvara* means guarding the six sense-doors—eyes, ears, nose, tongue, body and mind. *Bhojane mattaññutā* means taking just sufficient food to preserve the balance of the corporeality group in the body and being satisfied with that. *Jāgariyānuyogo* means not sleeping during the day, and sleeping only during one period (of the three periods) of the night and practising *bhāvanā* (mental concentration) during the other two periods.

The seven *saddhammas* are

1. *Saddhā* (faith)
2. *Sati* (mindfulness)
3. *Hiri* (moral shame)
4. *Ottappa* (moral dread)
5. *Bāhusacca* (great learning)
6. *Viriya* (energy; diligence)
7. *Paññā* (wisdom)

For those who wish to become *sotāpannas* during this life there is no special necessity to practice *dāna*. But let those who find themselves unable to evoke sufficient effort towards acquiring the ability to obtain release from worldly ills during the present Buddha Sāsana make special attempts to practice *dāna* and *uposatha-sīla* (precepts observed on Uposatha days).

Order of Practice and Those Who Await the Next Buddha

Since the work in the case of those who depend on and await the next Buddha consists of no more than acquiring accumulation of *pāramī*, it is not strictly necessary for them to adhere to the order of the stages of practice laid down in the Pāli texts, viz, *sīla*, *samādhi* and *paññā*. They should not thus defer the practice of *samādhi* before the completion of the practice of *sīla*, or defer the practice of *paññā* before the completion of the practice of *samādhi* In accordance with the order of the seven *visuddhis* (purifications), which are (1) *sīla-visuddhi* (purification of virtue), (2) *citta-visuddhi* (purification of mind),(3) *diṭṭhi-visuddhi* (purification of view), (4) *kaṅkhāvitaraṇa-visuddhi* (purification by overcoming doubt), (5)*maggāmagga-ñāṇadassana-visuddhi* (purification by knowledge and vision of what is and what is not path), (6) *paṭipadā-ñāṇadassana-visuddhi* (purification by knowledge and vision of the way), and (7) *ñāṇadassana-visuddhi* (purification by knowledge and vision), they should not postpone the practice of any course for a *visuddhi* until the completion of the respective previous course. Since they are persons engaged in the accumulation of as much of the seeds of *pāramī* as they can, they should contrive to accumulate the largest amount of *sīla*, *samādhi*, and *paññā*, that lies in their power.

When it is stated in the Pāli texts that *citta-visuddhi* should be practiced only after the completion of the practice of *sīla-visuddhi*, that *diṭṭhi-visuddhi* should be practiced only after the completion of the practice of *citta-visuddhi*, that *kaṅkhāvitaraṇa-visuddhi* should be practiced only after the completion of the practice of *diṭṭhi-visuddhi*, that the work of *anicca-*, *dukkha-*, and anattā-*bhāvanā* (contemplation of impermanence, suffering and impersonality) should be undertaken only after the completion of the practice of *kaṅkhāvitaraṇa-visuddhi*—the order of practice prescribed is meant for those who attempt the speedy realization of the paths and the fruits thereof in this very life. Since those who find themselves unable to call forth such effort, and are engaged only in the accumulation of the seeds of *pāramī*, are persons occupied in grasping whatever they can of good practices, it should not be said in their case that the work of *samatha-manasikāra-citta-visuddhi* (the practice of purification of mind consisting of advertence of mind to tranquillity) should not be undertaken before the fulfilment of *sīla-visuddhi*.

Even in the case of hunters and fishermen, it should not be said that they should not practice *samatha-vipassanā-manasikāra* (advertence of mind towards tranquility and insight) unless they discard their work. One who says so causes *dhammantarāya* (obstruction to the Dhamma). Hunters and fishermen should, on the other hand, be encouraged to contemplate the noble qualities of the Buddha, the Dhamma, and the Saṅgha. They should be induced to contemplate, as much as is in their power, the characteristic of loathsomeness in one's body. They should be urged to contemplate the liability of oneself and all creatures to death. I have come across the case of a leading fisherman who, as a result of such encouragement, could repeat fluently from memory the Pāli text and *nissaya* (word for word translation) of the *Abhidhammattha-saṅgaha*, and the *Paccaya Niddesa* of the *Paṭṭhāna* (Book of Relations), while still following the profession of a fisherman. These accomplishments constitute very good foundations for the acquisition of *vijjā*.

At the present time, whenever I meet my *dāyaka upāsakās* (lay disciples who contribute to a bhikkhu's upkeep), I tell them, in the true tradition of a bhikkhu, that even though they are hunters and fishermen by profession, they should be ever mindful of the noble qualities of the Three Jewels and the three characteristics of existence. To be mindful of the noble qualities of the *Tiratana* constitutes the seed of *caraṇa*. To be mindful of the three characteristics of existence constitutes the seed of *vijjā*. Even hunters and fishermen should be encouraged to practice those advertences of mind. They should not be told that it is improper for hunters and fishermen to practice advertence of mind towards *samatha* (tranquillity) and *vipassanā* (insight). On the other hand, they should be helped towards better understanding, should they be in difficulties. They should be urged and encouraged to keep on trying. They are in that stage when even the work of accumulating *pāramīs* and good tendencies is to be extolled.

Loss of Opportunity to Attain the Seed of *Vijjā* through Ignorance of the Value of the Present Times

Some teachers, who are aware only of the existence of direct and unequivocal statements in the Pāli texts regarding the order of practice of the seven *visuddhis*, but who take no account of the value of the present moment, say that in the practices of *samatha* and *vipassanā* no results can be achieved unless *sīla-visuddhi* is first fulfilled, whatever be the intensity of the effort. Some of the uninformed ordinary folk are beguiled by such statements. Thus has the *dhammantarāya* (obstruction to the Dhamma) occurred.

These persons, because they do not know the nature of the present moment, will lose the opportunity to attain the seeds of *vijjā*, which are attainable only when a Buddha Sāsana is encountered. In truth, they have not yet attained release from worldly ills and are still drifting in *saṃsāra* (round of rebirths) because, though they have occasionally encountered Buddha Sāsanas in their past inconceivably long saṃsāra, where Buddha Sāsanas more numerous than the grains of sands on the banks of the Ganges have appeared, they did not acquire the foundation of the seeds of *vijjā*.

When seeds are spoken of, there are seeds ripe or mature enough to sprout into healthy and strong seedlings, and there are many degrees of ripeness or maturity.

There are also seeds that are unripe or immature. People who do not know the meaning of the passages they recite or who do not know the right methods of practice even though they know the meaning, and who thus by custom or tradition read, recite, and count their beads while performing the work of contemplating the noble qualities of the Buddha and *anicca*, *dukkha* and *anattā*, possess seeds that are unripe and immature. These unripe seeds may be ripened and matured by the continuation of such work in the existences that follow, if opportunity for such continued work occurs.

The practice of *samatha* until the appearance of *parikamma- nimitta*[31] and the practice of *vipassanā* until insight is obtained into

31 *Nimitta* is the mental image which arises in the mind by the successful practice of certain concentration exercises. The image physically perceived at the very beginning of concentration is called the preparatory image or *parikamma-nimitta*.

rūpa and *nāma* (matter and mind) even once, are mature seeds filled with pith and substance. The practice of *samatha* until the appearance of *uggaha-nimitta*[32] and the practice of *vipassanā* until the acquisition of *sammasana-ñāṇa*[33] even once, are seeds that are still more mature. The practice of *samatha* until the appearance of *paṭibhāga-nimitta*,[34] and the practice of *vipassanā* until the occurrence of *udayabbaya-ñāṇa*[35] even once, are seeds that are yet more highly mature. If further higher efforts can be made in both *samatha* and *vipassanā*, still more mature seeds can obtained bringing great success.

Assiduous and Successful Practice (*Adhikāra*)

When it is said in the Pāli texts that only when there has been *adhikāra* in previous Buddha Sāsanas, can corresponding *jhānas*, the paths and the fruits be obtained in the following Buddha Sāsanas. Thus the word *adhikāra* means "successful seeds". Nowadays, those who pass their lives with traditional practices that are but imitation *samatha* and imitation *vipassanā* do not come within the purview of persons who possess the seeds of *samatha* and *vijjā* which can be called *adhikāra*.

Of the two kinds of seeds, those people who encounter a Buddha Sāsana, but who fail to secure the seeds of *vijjā*, suffer great loss indeed. This is so because the seeds of *vijjā* which are related to *rūpa*- and *nāma-dhammā* (bodily and mental processes) can only be obtained within a Buddha Sāsana, and that only when one is sensible

---

32 The still unsteady and unclear image which arises after the mind has reached a certain degree of concentration is called acquired image or *uggaha-nimitta*. This is solely a mental image.

33 Observing, exploring, grasping, determining all phenomena of existence as impermanent, miserable, and impersonal, which precedes the flashing up of clear insight.

34 The fully clear and immovable image that arises at a greater degree of concentration is called the counter-image or *paṭibhāga-nimitta*. This also is a mental image.

35 Knowledge arising from the contemplation of arising and vanishing. It is the first of the nine insight knowledges constituting the *paṭipadā-ñāṇadassana-visuddhi* (purification by knowledge and vision of the way).

enough to secure them. Hence, at the present time, those men and women who find themselves unable to contemplate and investigate at length into the nature of *rūpa*-and *nāma-dhamma*, should throughout their lives undertake the task of committing the four great primaries to memory, then of contemplating on their meaning and discussing them, and lastly of seeking insight into how they are constituted in their bodies.

Here ends the part showing, by a discussion of four classes of individuals and three kinds of individuals as given in the Sutta and *Abhidhamma Piṭakas*, that (1) those persons who within the Buddha Sāsana do not practice *samatha* and *vipassanā* but allow the time to pass with imitations, suffer great loss as they fail to utilize the unique opportunity arising from their existence as human beings within a Buddha Sāsana; (2) this being the time of *padaparama* and *neyya* classes of persons, if they heedfully put forth effort, they can secure ripe and mature seeds of *samatha* and *vipassanā*, and easily attain the supramundane benefit either within this life or in the *deva loka* (*deva* abodes) in the next life—within this Buddha Sāsana or within the Sāsana or the next Buddha; (3) they can derive immense benefit from their existence as human beings during the Buddha Sāsana.

Here ends the exposition of the three kinds and the four kinds of individuals.

A Word of Advice and Warning

If the Tipiṭaka which contains the discourses of the Buddha delivered during forty-five *vassas* (rainy seasons) be condensed, and the essentials extracted, the thirty-seven *bodhipakkhiya-dhammas* (requisites of enlightenment) are obtained. These thirty-seven *bodhipakkhiya-dhamma* constitute the essence of the Tipiṭaka. If these be further condensed, the seven *visuddhis* are obtained. If again the seven *visuddhis* be condensed, they become *sīla*, *samādhi*, and *paññā* (wisdom). These are called *adhisīla-sāsana* (the teaching of higher morality), *adhicitta-sāsana* (the teaching of higher mentality), and *adhipaññā-sāsana* (the teaching of higher wisdom). They are also called the three *sikkhās* (trainings).

When *sīla* is mentioned, the essential for laymen is *nicca-sīla*. Those people who fulfil *nicca-sīla* become endowed with *caraṇa* which, with *vijjā*, enables them to attain the paths and the fruits. If these persons can add the refinement of *uposatha-sīla* over *nicca sīla*, it is much better. For laymen, *nicca-sīla* means *ājīvaṭṭhamaka-sīla*.[36] That *sīla* must be properly and faithfully kept. If because they are *puthujjanas* (worldlings) they break the *sīla*, it can be re-established immediately by renewing the undertaking to keep the *sīla* for the rest of their lives. If, on a future occasion, the *sīla* is again broken, it can again be similarly cleansed, and every time this cleansing occurs, the person concerned again becomes endowed with *sīla*. The effort is not difficult. Whenever *nicca-sīla* is broken, it should be immediately re-established. In these days, persons endowed with *sīla* abound in large numbers.

But such persons are very rare who have attained perfect concentration in one or other of the *kasiṇa* exercises, or in the practice of *asubha-bhāvanā* (meditation of loathsomeness), etc., as also are persons who have sometimes attained insight into physical and mental phenomena, the three characteristics, etc. Such persons are very rare because these are times when wrong teachings (*micchā-dhammā*) are ripe that are likely to cause *dhammantarāya*, (danger and obstruction to the Dhamma).

Wrong Teachings

By wrong teachings likely to cause obstruction to the Dhamma are meant such views, practices, and limitations as the inability to see the dangers of *saṃsāra*, the belief that these are times when the paths and the fruits can no longer be attained, the tendency to defer effort until the *pāramīs* ripen, the belief that persons of the present day are *dvi-hetuka*,[37] the belief that the great teachers of the past were non-existent, etc.

Even though it does not reach the ultimate, no *kusala-kamma* (wholesome volitional action) is ever rendered futile. If effort be made, a *kusala-kamma* is instrumental in producing *pāramī* in those

---

36 See note 20.

37 *Dvi-hetuka-paṭisandhi*. This refers to a rebirth with only two good root-conditions, viz. non-greed (*alobha*) and non-hate (*adosa*). Beings so reborn cannot attain the paths and fruitions in their present life, as they lack the third root-conditions, non-delusion (*amoha*).

who do not possess *pāramī*. If no effort be made, the opportunity to acquire *pāramī* is lost. If those whose *pāramīs* are immature put forth effort, their *pāramīs* become ripe and mature. Such persons can attain the paths and fruits in their next existence within the present Sāsana. If no effort be made, the opportunity for the *pāramī* to ripen is lost. If those whose *pāramī* is ripe and mature put forth effort, the paths and the fruits can be attained within this life. If no effort be made, the opportunity to attain the paths and the fruits is lost.

If persons who are *dvi-hetuka* put forth effort, they can become *ti-hetuka*[38] in their next existence. If they do not put forth effort, they cannot ascend from the stage of *dvi-hetuka* and will slide down to the stage of *ahetuka*.[39] Suppose there is a certain person who plans to become a bhikkhu. If another person says to him, "Entertain the intention only if you can remain a monk all your life. Otherwise do not entertain the idea"—this would amount to *dhammantarāya*, an obstruction of Dhamma.

The Buddha said: "I declare that the mere arising of an intention of performing good deeds is productive of great benefit" (MN 8).

To disparage either the act of *dāna* (alms-giving) or to discourage the performer of *dāna*, may invoke *puññantarāya* on such a person, i.e., he causes obstruction to the performance of meritorious actions. If acts of morality, concentration (meditation) and wisdom, or those who perform them are disparaged, a *dhammantarāya* may be caused, i.e., an obstruction to Dhamma. If obstruction to meritorious actions is caused, one is liable to be bereft of power and influence, of property and riches and be abjectly poor, in the lives that follow. If obstruction to Dhamma is caused, one is liable to be defective in conduct and behavior and defective of sense, and thus be utterly low and debased in the existences that follow. Hence, let all beware!

Here ends the section showing how the rare opportunity of rebirth as a human being can be made worthwhile, by ridding oneself of the wrong Dhammas mentioned above, and putting forth effort in this life so as to close the gates of the four lower worlds (*apāya*) in one's future *saṃsāra* (round of rebirths), or else to accumulate the seeds that will enable one to attain release from worldly ills in the

38 *Tihetuka-paṭisandhi*: rebirth with all three good root-conditions *alobha, adosa, amoha*.

39 *Ahetuka*: a being reborn without any of the good root-conditions.

next following existence or within the next Buddha Sāsana, through the practice of tranquillity (*samatha*) and insight (*vipassanā*), with resolution, zeal and diligence.

CHAPTER I

THE REQUISITES OF ENLIGHTENMENT *(Bodhipakkhiya-dhamma)*

I shall now concisely describe the thirty-seven *bodhipakkhiya-dhammas*, the requisites of enlightenment,[40] which should be practiced with energy and determination by those persons who wish to cultivate tranquillity and insight and thus make worthwhile the rare opportunity of rebirth as a human being within the present Buddha Sāsana.

The *bodhipakkhiya dhammas* consist of seven groups, (totalling thirty-seven factors).

1. *Satipaṭṭhāna*, foundations of mindfulness (four factors)
2. *Sammāpadhāna*, right efforts (four factors)
3. *Iddhipāda*, bases of success (four factors)
4. *Indriya*, controlling faculties (five factors)
5. *Bala*, mental powers (five factors)
6. *Bojjhaṅga*, factors of enlightenment (seven factors)
7. *Maggaṅga*, path factors (eight factors)

The *bodhipakkhiya-dhammas* are so called because they form part (*pakkhiya*) of enlightenment or awakening (*bodhi*) which here refers to the knowledge of the holy paths (*magga-ñāṇa*). They are *dhammas* (mental phenomena) with the function of being proximate causes (*padaṭṭhāna*), requisite ingredients (*sambhāra*) and bases, or sufficient conditions (*upanissaya*), of path knowledge (*magga-ñāṇa*).

40 On this rendering see Editor's Preface.

CHAPTER II

THE FOUNDATIONS OF MINDFULNESS *(Satipaṭṭhāna)*

The word *satipaṭṭhāna* is defined as follows:

Bhusaṃ tiṭṭhati'ti paṭṭhānaṃ sati-paṭṭhānaṃ.

This means: "What is firmly established is a "foundation"; mindfulness itself is such a foundation."

There are four foundations of mindfulness:

1. *Kāyānupassanā-satipaṭṭhāna* (contemplation of the body as a foundation of mindfulness)
2. *Vedanānupassanā-satipaṭṭhāna* (contemplation of feelings as a foundation of mindfulness)
3. *Cittānupassanā-satipaṭṭhāna* (contemplation of the mind as a foundation of mindfulness)
4. *Dhammānupassanā-satipaṭṭhāna* (contemplation of mind-objects as a foundation of mindfulness)

1. *Kāyānupassanā-satipaṭṭhāna* means mindfulness which is firmly established on bodily phenomena, such as inhalation and exhalation.

2. *Vedanānupassanā-satipaṭṭhāna* means mindfulness which is firmly established on feelings (sensations).

3. *Cittānupassanā-satipaṭṭhāna* means mindfulness which is firmly established on thoughts or mental processes, such as thoughts associated with passions or dissociated from passions.

4. *Dhammānupassanā-satipātthāna* means mindfulness which is firmly established on phenomena such as hindrances (*nivaraṇa*), etc.

Of the four, if mindfulness or attention is firmly establish part of the body, such as on out-breath and in-breath, it is tantan to attention being firmly established on all things. This is beca the ability to place one's attention on any object at one's will h been acquired.

"Firmly established" means, if one desires to place the attention on the out-breath and in-breath for an hour, one's attention remains firmly fixed on it for that period. If one wishes to do so for two hours, one's attention remains firmly fixed on it for two hours. There is no occasion when the attention becomes released from its object on account of the instability of thought-conception (*vitakka*).

For a detailed account of the *satipaṭṭhāna*, see the Satipaṭṭhāna Sutta.[41]

Why is it incumbent on us to firmly establish the mind without fail on any object such as the out-breath and the in-breath? It is because it is necessary for us to gather and control the six types of consciousness (*viññāṇa*),[42] which have been drifting tempestuously and untrained throughout the past inconceivably long and beginningless *saṃsāra*.

I shall make it clearer. The mind tends to flit about from one to another of the six objects of the senses which lie at the approaches of the six sense-doors.[43]

As an example, take the case of a madman who has no control over his mind. He does not even know the mealtime, and wanders about aimlessly from place to place. His parents look for him and give him his meal. After eating five or six morsels of food he overturns the dish and walks away. He thus fails to get a square meal. To this extent he has lost control of his mind. He cannot control his mind even to the extent of finishing the business of a meal. In talking, he cannot control his mind to the extent of finishing or completing a sentence. The beginning, the middle, and the end do not agree with one another. His talk has no meaning. He cannot be of use in any undertaking in this world. He is unable to perform any task.

41 Transl. in *The Wheel* No. 18—See also the commentary to this sutta in *The Way of Mindfulness*, tr. by Soma Thera (Buddhist Publication Society, Kandy).

42 Eye-, ear-, nose-, tongue-, body- and mind-consciousness.

43 Eye-door, etc.

be classed as a human being, and he has

ane and normal person again, if he
doctor applies a cure. Thus cured he
mind in the matter of taking his meals, and
l. He has control over his mind in all other matters
can perform his tasks till they are completed, just like
s. Just like others, he can also complete his sentences. This is an example.

In this world, persons who are not insane but who are normal and have control over their minds, resemble such a mad person who has no control over his mind when it comes to the matter of *samatha* and *vipassanā*. Just as the madman upsets the food dish and walks away after five or six morsels of food, although he attempts to eat his meal, these normally sane persons find their attention wandering because they have no control over their minds. Whenever they pay respects to the Buddha and contemplate his noble qualities, they do not succeed in keeping their minds fixed on those noble qualities, but find their attention being diverted many times on to other objects of thought, and thus they even fail to reach the end of "*Iti pi so*" (a devotional text, beginning with these words, i.e., "Thus indeed is this Exalted One …").

It is as if a man suffering from hydrophobia who seeks water feverishly with parched lips, runs away from it with fear when he sees a lake of cool refreshing water. It is also like a diseased man who, when given a diet of relishing food replete with medicinal qualities, finds the food bitter to his taste and, unable to swallow it, is obliged to spit and vomit it out. In just the same way, these persons find themselves unable to approach the contemplation of the noble qualities of the Buddha effectively, and cannot maintain dwelling on them.

If in reciting the "*Iti pi so*" their recitation is interrupted every time their minds wander, and if they have to start afresh from the beginning every time such an interruption occurs, they will never reach the end of the text even though they keep on reciting a whole day, or a whole month, or a whole year. At present they manage to reach the end because they can keep on reciting from memory even though their minds wander elsewhere.

In the same way, there are persons who, on Uposatha days, plan to go to quiet places in order to contemplate the thirty-two parts of the body, such as *kesā* (hairs of the head), *lomā* (hairs of the body), etc. or the noble qualities of the Buddha, but who ultimately end up in the company of friends and associates because they have no control over their minds, and because of the upheavals in their thoughts and intentions. When they take part in congregational recitations, although they attempt to direct their minds to the *samatha* work of the *brahma-vihāras* (sublime states),[44] such as reciting the formula for diffusing *mettā* (loving kindness), because they have no control over their minds, their thoughts are not concentrated but are scattered aimlessly, and they end up only with the external manifestation of the recitation.

These facts are sufficient to show how many persons resemble the insane while performing *kusala-kammas*.

Pāpasmiṃ ramate mano

The mind takes delight in evil. (Dhp 116)

Just as water naturally flows down from high places to low places, the minds of beings, if left uncontrolled, naturally approach evil. This is the tendency of the mind.

I shall now draw, with examples, a comparison between those who exercise no control over their minds and the insane person mentioned above.

There is a river with a swift current. A boatman not familiar with the control of the rudder, floats down the river with the current. His boat is loaded with valuable merchandise for trading and selling at the towns on the lower reaches of the river. As he floats down, he passes stretches of the river lined with mountains and forests where there are no harbours or anchorages for his boat. He thus continues to float down without stopping. When night descends, he passes towns and village with harbours and anchorages, but he does not see

---

44 The four sublime states, namely *mettā* (loving kindness), *karuṇā* (compassion), *muditā* (altruistic joy), and *upekkhā* (equanimity). See *The Wheel* No. 6.

them in the darkness of the night, and thus he continues to float without stopping. When daylight arrives, he comes to places with towns and villages, but not having any control over the rudder of the boat, he cannot steer it to the harbors and anchorages, and thus, inevitably, he continues to float down until he reaches the great wide ocean.

The infinitely lengthy *saṃsāra* is like the swift-flowing river. Beings having no control over their minds are like the boatman who is unable to steer his boat. The mind is like the boat. Beings who have drifted from one existence to another in the "*suñña*" world-cycles, where no Buddha Sāsanas appear, are like the boatman drifting down those stretches of the river lined by mountains and forests, where there are no harbours and anchorages. When at times these beings are born in world-cycles where Buddha Sāsanas flourish, but are in ignorance of them because they happen to be in one or other of the eight *aṭṭhakkhaṇas* (inopportune situations), they resemble the boatman who floats down stretches of the river lined by towns and villages with harbours and anchorages, but does not see them because it is night. When, at other times, they are born as human beings, *devas* or *brahmas*, within a Buddha Sāsana, but fail to secure the paths and the fruits because they are unable to control their minds and put forth effort to practice *vipassanā* exercises of the *satipaṭṭhānas* thus continuing still to drift in *saṃsāra*, they resemble the boatman who sees the banks lined by towns and villages with harbours and anchorages, but is unable to steer towards them because of his inability to control the rudder, and thus continues inevitably to drift down towards the ocean. In the infinitely lengthy *saṃsāra*, those beings who have obtained release from worldly ills within the Sāsanas of the Buddhas who have appeared, whose numbers exceed the grains of sand on the banks of the river Ganges, are beings who had control over their minds and who possessed the ability of retaining their attention on any desired object at will through the practice of the *satipaṭṭhānas*.

This shows the trend of the wandering, or "course of existence," of those beings who do not practice the *satipaṭṭhānas*, even though they are aware of the fact that they have no control over their minds when it comes to the practice of *samatha* and *vipassanā*.

Comparisons may also be made with the taming and training of bullocks for the purpose of yoking them to ploughs and carts, and to the taming and training of elephants for employment in the service of the king, or on battlefields.

In the case of the bullock, the young calf has to be regularly herded and kept in a cattle-pen, then a nose rope is passed through its nostrils and it is tied to a post and trained to respond to the rope's control. It is then trained to submit to the yoke, and only when it becomes amenable to the yoke's burden is it put to use for ploughing and drawing carts and thus effectively employed to trade and profit. This is the example of the bullock.

In this example, just as the owner's profit and success depends on the employment of the bullock in the drawing of ploughs and carts after training it to become amenable to the yoke, so does the true benefit of lay persons and bhikkhus within the present Sāsana depend on training in *samatha* and *vipassanā*

In the present Buddha Sāsana, the practice of *sīla-visuddhi* resembles the training of the young calf by herding it and keeping it in cattle-pens. Just as, if the young calf is not so herded and kept in cattle pens, it would damage and destroy the properties of others and thus bring liability on the owner, so, too, if a person lacks *sīla-visuddhi*, the three (unwholesome) *kammas*[45] would run riot, and the person concerned would become subject to worldly evils and to the evil results indicated in the Dhamma.

The efforts to develop *kāyagatāsati*[46] resembles the passing of the nose-rope through the nostrils and training the calf to respond to the rope after tying it to a post. Just as when a calf is tied to a post it can be kept wherever the owner desires it to be, and it cannot run loose, so when the mind is tied to the body with the rope of *satipaṭṭhāna*, that mind cannot wander but is obliged to remain

---

45 The ten unwholesome actions:

Kāya-kamma: threefold unwholesome bodily actions of killing, stealing, improper sexual intercourse;

Vacī-kamma: fourfold unwholesome verbal actions of lying, slandering, rude speech, foolish babble;

Mano-kamma: threefold unwholesome mental actions of avarice, ill will, and wrong views.

46 Mindfulness with regard to the body.

wherever the owner desires it to be. The habits of a disturbed and distracted mind acquired during the inconceivably long *saṃsāra*, become weakened.

A person who performs the practice of *samatha* and *vipassanā* without first attempting body-contemplation, resembles the owner who yokes the still untamed bullock to the cart or plough without the nose-rope. Such an owner would find himself unable to control the bullock as he desires. Because the bullock is wild, and because it has no nose-rope, it will either try to run off the road, or try to break loose by breaking the yoke.

On the other hand, a person who first tranquilizes and trains his mind with body contemplation before turning his mind to the practice of *samatha* and *vipassanā* will find that his attention will remain steady and his work will be successful.

In the case of the elephant, the wild elephant has first to be brought out from the forest into the field hitched on to a tame, trained elephant. Then it is taken to a stockade and tied up securely until it is tamed. When it thus becomes absolutely tame and quiet, it is trained in the various kinds of work in which it will be employed in the service of the king. It is only then that it is used in state functions and on battlefields.

The realm of sensual pleasures resembles the forest where the wild elephant enjoys himself. The Buddha Sāsana resembles the open field into which the wild elephant is first brought out. The mind resembles the wild elephant. Faith (*saddhā*) and desire (*chanda*) in the *sāsana-dhamma* resemble the tame, trained elephant to which the wild elephant is hitched and brought out into the open. *Sīla-visuddhi* (purification of virtue) resembles the stockade. The body, or parts of the body, such as out-breath and in-breath resemble the post in the stockade to which the elephant is tied. *Kāyagatāsati*[47] resembles the rope by which the wild elephant is tied to the post. The preparatory work towards *samatha* and *vipassanā* resembles the preparatory training of the elephant. The work of *samatha* and *vipassanā* resembles the king's parade ground or the battlefield. Other points of comparison can also be easily recognized.

---

47 "Mindful contemplation directed at the body." In the following called, for short, "body contemplation."

Thus I have shown by the examples of the mad man, the boatman, the bullock, and the elephant, the main points of body contemplation, which is by ancient tradition the first step that has to be undertaken in the work of proceeding upwards from *sīla-visuddhi* within the Sāsanas of all the Buddhas who have appeared in the past inconceivably long *saṃsāra*.

The essential meaning is that, whether it be by out-breathing and in-breathing, or by *iriyāpatha* (four postures: going, standing, sitting, lying) or by *sampajañña* (clear comprehension) or by *dhātu-manasikāra* (advertence of mind on the elements) or by *aṭṭhika-saññā* (contemplation of bones), one must put forth effort in order to acquire the ability of placing one's attention on one's body and its postures for as long as one wishes throughout the day and night at all waking hours. If one can keep one's attention fixed for as long as one wishes, then mastery has been obtained over one's mind. Thus does one attain release from the state of a mad man. One now resembles the boatman who has obtained mastery over his rudder, or the owner of the tamed and trained bullock, or the king who employs the tamed and trained elephant.

There are many kinds, and many grades, of mastery over the mind. The successful practice of body contemplation is, in the Buddha Sāsana, the first stage of mastery over one's mind.

Those who do not wish to follow the way of *samatha* but desire to pursue the path of pure *vipassanā* which is the way of the *sukkha-vipassaka*[48] individual, should proceed straight to *vipassanā* after the successful establishment of body contemplation.

If they do not want to practice body contemplation separately and if they mean to practice insight with such industry that it may carry *kāyagatāsati* with it, they will succeed, provided that they really have the necessary wisdom and industry. The body contemplation (*kāyagatāsati*) that is associated with *udayabbaya-ñāṇa* (knowledge arising from contemplation of the arisings and vanishings of mental and physical phenomena), which clearly sees their coming into existence and passing away, is very valuable indeed.

In the *samatha* method, by practising the body contemplation of out- and in-breathing, one can attain up to *rūpāvacara-catuttha-jhāna*

48 One who practices *vipassanā* (insight) only.

(the fourth *jhāna* of the form sphere); by practising *vaṇṇa-manasikāra*[49] of the *kāyagatāsati* of the thirty-two parts of the body, such as *kesā* (hair of the head), *lomā* (hair of the body), etc., one can attain all the eight *samāpattis*,[50] and by practising *paṭik-kūla-manasikāra*[51] of the same body contemplation one can attain the first *jhāna*. If *vipassanā* is attained in the process, one also can attain the paths and the fruits.

Even if completion is not arrived at in the practice of *samatha* and *vipassanā*, if the stage is reached where one attains control over one's mind and the ability to keep one's attention fixed on wherever one wishes it to be, it was said by the Buddha that such a one can be said to be one who enjoys the flavour of *amata* or *nibbāna*.[52]

> *Amataṃ tesaṃ paribhuttaṃ, yesaṃ kāyagatāsati paribhuttā.*[53]
>
> Those who enjoy body contemplation (*kāyagatāsati*), enjoy the Deathless (*amata*).

Here, *amata* means great peacefulness or tranquillity of mind.[54]

In its original untamed state, the mind is highly unstable in its attentiveness, and thus is parched and hot in its nature. Just as the insects that live on capsicum are not aware of its heat, just as beings pursuing the realm of *taṇhā* (craving) are not aware of *taṇhā's* heat, just as beings subject to anger and pride are not aware of the heat of pride and anger, so are beings unaware of the heat of unsettled minds. It is only when, through *kāyagatā*sati, the unsettled condition of the mind disappears, that they become aware of the heat of an unsettled mind. Having attained the state of the disappearance of that heat, they develop a fear of a relapse to that heat. The case of those who have attained the first *jhāna*, or knowledge of rise and fall

---

49 Attention to the color or appearance, which is a part of the meditation of the thirty-two parts of the body.

50 The four meditative absorptions (*jhāna*) of the form sphere and the four of the formless sphere.

51 Contemplation of Loathsomeness.

52 The Deathless—a term for Nibbāna.

53 AN 1:21.49 *Ekaka-nipāta*.

54 This refers to *kilesa-nibbāna*, the "extinction of the defilements" during the lifetime of the arahat.

(*udayabbaya-ñāṇa*) through body contemplation (*kāyagatā-satipaṭṭhāna*), needs no elaboration.

Hence, the higher the attainments that one reaches, the more difficult does it become for one to be apart from *kāyagatāsati*. The *ariya-puggalas* (holy ones) use the four *satipaṭṭhānas* as mental nutriment until they attain Parinibbāna.

The ability to keep one's attention fixed on parts of the body, such as out-breath, and in-breath for one or two hours takes one to the culmination of one's work in seven days, or fifteen days, or a month, or two months, or three months, or four months, or five months, or six months, or a year, or two years, or four years, according to the intensity of one's efforts.

For the method of practising out-breathing and in-breathing, see my *Ānāpāna Dīpanī*[55]

There are many books by past teachers on the method of the thirty-two parts of the body. In this method, *kesā* (hair of the head), *lomā* (hair of the body), *nakhā* (nails), *dantā* (teeth), *taco* (skin) are known as *taca-pañcaka* (group ending with taco as the fifth). If attention can be firmly fixed on these five, the work of *kāyagatāsati* (body contemplation) is accomplished.

For *catu-dhātu-vavatthāna* (analysis of the four great primaries), *rūpa-vipassanā* (contemplation of physical phenomena), and *nāma-vipassanā* (contemplation of mental phenomena), see my *Lakkhaṇa Dīpanī*, *Vijjāmagga Dīpanī*, *Ahāra Dīpanī* and *Anattā Dīpanī*[56].

Here ends a concise explanation of *kāyagatāsati-bhāvanā*, which is one of the four *satipaṭṭhānas*, and which has to be established first in the work of *bhāvanā* (mental contemplation) by *neyya* and *padaparama* individuals for the purpose of attaining the paths and the fruits within a Buddha Sāsana.

---

55 Translated as *Manual of Mindfulness of Breathing*, *The Wheel* No. 431/432 B.P.S. See also *Mindfulness of Breathing*, by Ñāṇamoli Thera (BPS, Kandy) for a work covering this subject.

56 Some of these works are still not available in English translation.

CHAPTER III

The Four Right Efforts
(Sammāpadhāna)

The word *sammāpadhāna* is defined as follows:

> *Bhusaṃ dahati vahati'ti padhānaṃ sammadeva padhānaṃ sammāpadhānaṃ.*

This means: *padhāna* is an effort carried out strongly, intensively; if carried out properly, rightly, it is *sammāpadhāna*, right effort.

It is an effort that has not in it any element of unwillingness. It is also called "zealous energy" (*ātāpaviriya*). It is an effort that has the four characteristics spoken of in the following text:

> *Kāmaṃ taco ca nahāru ca aṭṭhi ca avasissatu, sarīre upasussatu maṃsalohitaṃ; yaṃ taṃ purisathāmena purisaviriyena purisaparakkamena pattabbaṃ, na taṃ apapuṇitvā viriyassa saṇṭhānaṃ bhavissati.*
>
> "Let only my skin, and sinews, and bones remain and let my flesh and blood in the body dry up, I shall not permit the course of my effort to stop until I win that which may be won by human ability, human effort and human exertion". (AN 2:1.5)

These characteristics may be summed up as follows:

1. Let the skin remain,
2. Let the sinews remain,
3. Let the bones remain,
4. Let the flesh and blood dry up.

It is the effort that calls forth the determination, "If the end is attainable by human effort, I shall not rest or relax until it is attained, until the end is grasped and reached." It is the effort of the kind put forth by the Venerable bhikkhu Soṇa[57] and the Venerable Cakkhupāla.[58]

It is only when the *jhāna*, the paths, and the fruits are not attained after effort is put forth on this scale, as prescribed by the Buddha and throughout one's life, that it can it be said that the cause (of the failure) lies in the nature of the present times, or in one being *dvi-hetuka*, or in one's lack of sufficient previously accumulated *pāramī*.

In this world, some persons, far from putting forth the full scale of the effort prescribed by the Buddha, do not even try to set up body contemplation effectively in order to cure their minds of aimless drifting, and yet they say that their failure to attain the paths and the fruits is due to the fact that these are times that preclude such attainment. There are others of the same class who say that men and women of the present day have not the necessary accumulation of *pāramī* (perfections) to enable them to attain the paths and the fruits. There are yet others of the same class who say that men and women of the present day are *dvi-hetuka*. All these people say so because they do not know that these are times of the *neyya* class of individuals who fail to attain the paths and the fruits because they are lacking in *sammāpadhāna* effort.

If proper *sammāpadhāna* effort be put forth with dedicated intention (*pahitatta*) where a thousand put forth effort, three, four, or five hundred of them can attain the supreme achievement; if a hundred put forth effort, thirty, forty, or fifty of them can attain the supreme achievement. Here, *pahitatta*, intention, means "determination to adhere to the effort throughout one's life and to die, if need be, while still making the effort."

The Venerable Soṇa Thera's effort consisted of keeping awake throughout the three months of the *vassa* (rainy season), the only body postures adopted being sitting and walking. The Venerable Cakkhupāla's effort was of the same order. The Venerable Phussadeva Thera[59] achieved the paths and the fruits only after twenty-five

---

57 Vinaya Piṭaka, Mahāvagga, V.13. *Sammohavinodani* (Commentary: to Paṭisambhidāmagga).

58 Dhammapada Commentary; story relating to verse 1.

59 See Comy. to Satipaṭṭhāna Sutta.

years of the same order of effort. In the case of the Venerable Mahāsiva[60] Thera the effort lasted thirty years.

At the present day, there is a great need for such kind of *sammāpadhāna* effort. It happens that those who put forth the effort have not sufficient foundations in the *pariyatti* (learning of the doctrine), while those who possess sufficient *pariyatti* foundations live involved in the *palibodhas* (obstacles) of the business of bhikkhus; according as they live in towns and villages these include such matters as discussing the Dhamma, delivering sermons and discourses, and writing books on the Dhamma. They are persons who are unable to put forth *sammāpadhāna* effort for lengthy periods without a break.

Some persons are inclined to say that when their *pāramīs* become ripe for them to attain release from worldly ills they can easily obtain that release and that, as such, they cannot put forth effort now when they are not certain whether or not that effort will result in release. They do not appear to compare the suffering occasioned by thirty years' effort now with the suffering they will encounter if, in the interim before they attain release, they are cast in the hell regions for a hundred thousand years. They do not appear to remember that the suffering occasioned by thirty years' effort is not as bad as the suffering caused by just three hours in the hell regions.

They may say that the situation will be the same if no release is attained after thirty years' effort, i.e., they will be no closer to release. But if the person is sufficiently mature for release, they will attain that release through that effort. If they are not sufficiently mature, they will attain release in the next life. Even if they fail to attain release within the present Buddha Sāsana, the *kamma* of repeated efforts at mental development (*bhāvanā-āciṇṇa-kamma*) is a powerful *kamma*. Through it one can avoid the *apāya* regions, and can meet the next Buddha after continuous rebirths in the *sugati* existence (happy course of existence). In the case of those who do not put forth the effort, they will miss the opportunity of release even though they are mature enough to obtain release through thirty years' effort. For lack of effort they have nothing to gain and everything to lose. Let all, therefore, acquire the eye of wisdom, and beware of the danger of not making effort.

---

60 See Comy. to Sakkapañha Sutta (DN).

There are four kinds of *sammāpadhāna*,[61] namely:

1. *Uppannānaṃ akusalānaṃ dhammānaṃ pahānāya vāyāmo.*
2. *Anuppannānaṃ akusalānaṃ dhammānaṃ anuppādāya vāyāmo*
3. *Anuppannānaṃ kusalānaṃ dhammānaṃ uppādāya vāyāmo*
4. *Uppannānaṃ kusalānaṃ dhammānaṃ bhiyyobhāvāya vāyāmo*

1. Effort to overcome or reject evil unwholesome acts that have arisen, or are in the course of arising
2. Effort to avoid (not only in this life but also in the lives that follow) the arising of unwholesome acts that have not yet arisen
3. Effort to arouse the arising of wholesome acts that have not yet arisen
4. Effort to increase and to perpetuate the wholesome acts that have arisen or are in the course of arising

Arisen and Not Arisen Unwholesome Acts *(Uppanna* and *Anuppanna Akusala Kamma)*

In the personality of every being wandering in *saṃsāra*, there are two kinds of *akusala-kammas* (unwholesome volitional actions), namely,

1. *Uppanna-akusala-kamma*
2. *Anuppanna-akusala-kamma*

Uppanna-akusala-kamma (arisen unwholesome acts) means past and present *akusala-kammas*. They comprise unwholesome volitional actions committed in the interminable series of past world-cycles and past lives. Among these *akusala-kammas*, there are some that have spent themselves by having produced rebirths in the *apāya-lokas* (the four low and miserable regions of existence). There are others that await the opportunity of producing rebirths in the *apāya-lokas*, and thus constitute potentialities for rebirth in the

61 See Aṅguttara Nikāya., The Fours, No. 13ff. *"The Book of Analysis"* (*Vibhanga*), tr. by U Thittila (Pali Text Society, London), p. 271ff.

apāya-lokas that accompany beings from world-cycle to world-cycle and from life to life.

Every being in whom *sakkāya-diṭṭhi* (personality-belief) resides, be he a human being, or a *deva*, or *brahmā*, possesses an infinitely large store of such past debts, so to say, consisting of *akusala-kammas* that have in them the potentiality of producing rebirths in the lowest *avīci* hell. Similarly, there are infinite stores of other *kammas* capable of producing rebirths in the other *apāya-lokas*. These past *kammas* which await a favorable opportunity for producing rebirth resultants and which accompany beings from life to life until they are expended, are called *uppanna*.

These past *uppanna-akusala-kammas* have their roots in *sakkāya-diṭṭhi*. As long as *sakkāya-diṭṭhi* exists, they are not expended without producing resultants. But when, with insight into the *anatta-lakkhaṇa* (characteristic of impersonality), one rids oneself of *sakkāya-diṭṭhi*, from that instant all the *uppanna-akusala-kammas* lose their potentiality and disappear from the store of past *akusala-kammas*. From that existence, one will no longer become subject to rebirth in the *apāya-lokas* in future *saṃsāra* not even in one's dreams.

Anuppanna-akusala-kammas means future *akusala-kammas*. Beginning with the next instant in this life, all the new evil and unwholesome acts that one commits whenever opportunity occurs in the course of this present life and in the succession of lives that are to follow, are called *anuppanna*. These new *akusala-duccarita-kammas* that one can commit even during a single lifetime can be infinite in number.

All these *anuppanna-akusala-kammas* have their origin in personality belief. If at any time personality-belief disappears, all the new *anuppanna-akusala-kammas* also disappear, even at that instant, from the personality of the beings concerned, leaving no residue. Here, "disappear" means that there will be no occasion, starting from the next instant, in the future succession of lives and the future succession of world-cycles, when new *akusala-kammas* are perpetrated. Throughout future *anamatagga-saṃsāra* (beginningless round of rebirths), those beings will not commit, even in their dreams, any *akusala-kamma* such as *pāṇātipāta* (killing any living being).

If personality-belief remains, even though the being is a Universal Monarch exercising sway over the whole universe, he is, as it were, sandwiched between hell-fires in front and hell-fires behind, and is thus hedged in between the two *akusala-kammas* of *uppanna* and *anuppanna*. He is thus purely a creature of hell-heat. Similarly, the kings of the *devalokas*, Sakkā the king of the *Tāvatiṃsa-devaloka*, the *Brahmās* of the *rūpa* and *arūpa*[62] *Brahma*-worlds, are all purely creatures of hell-heat. They are creatures that are hitched on to the chains of hell and the *apāya* regions. In the great whirlpool of *saṃsāra*, they are purely creatures who drift or sink.

In the infinitely long *saṃsāra*, beings have to cultivate the desire for encountering a Buddha Sāsana, which is an extremely difficult achievement. Hedged in as they are, from before and behind, by the hell-fires of *uppanna* and *anuppanna-akusala-kammas*, they have to cultivate earnestly the desire to extinguish those fires once and for all. Hence, those beings who do encounter Buddha Sāsanas have to make the extinguishing of the hell-fires of *uppanna* and *anuppanna* their sole task for their future welfare.

The task of extinguishing the unwholesome acts, arisen and not arisen consists of ridding oneself of *sakkāya-diṭṭhi* and no more. If *sakkāya-diṭṭhi* is uprooted, the two *akusala-kammas* are entirely extinguished.

Bon-sin-san *sotāpannas*[63], like Visākhā and Anāthapiṇḍika, who are infinitely numerous among humans, *devas*, and *brahmās*,

---

62 Fine-material and immaterial.

63 Bon-sin-san is a term in the Burmese language, signifying a type of stream-enterer *(sotāpanna)* that will reach final deliverance in Arahatship after numerous rebirths in successively higher stages of existences. This term has no equivalent in the sutta texts where only those are called *sotāpannas* who have, at the utmost, seven rebirths before them, among men and deities. Bon-sin-san is a concept familiar in Burmese doctrinal tradition, for which reference is made to the following commentarial passages which are said to imply the sense of the term:

Comy. to *Indriya-Saṃyutta, Chalindriya Vagga*, Ekabīji Sutta, commenting on the word *sattakkhattuparamo*. Comy. to Dīgha Nikāya, Sakkapañha Sutta (at the end), commenting on the words so *nivāso bhavissati*. Comy. to Puggala-paññatti (Pañcappakarana are beings who have obtained release from the state of sinking and drifting in the great whirlpool of *saṃsāra* (round of rebirths) from the moment *sakkāya-diṭṭhi* was uprooted. They are beings who have attained the first stage of Nibbāna called *sa-upādisesa-nibbāna* (Nibbāna with the five constituent groups of existence remaining)[64]. Although they are liable to wander in the round of rebirths for many more lives and many more world-cycles, they are no longer worldly

---

Aṭṭhakatha), Ekaka-niddesa, commenting on the word *ekabīji*.

For these references, and the following comments, the Editor is obliged to the Venerable Mahāsi Sayādaw, Agga-Mahā-Paṇḍita, of Rangoon:

(1) One becomes a *sotāpanna* in the *kāmabhūmi* (sense-sphere) and achieves the higher three stages (*sakadāgāmi*, etc.) in *suddhāvāsa* (five planes) of *rūpa loka* (fine material worlds), after sojourn in the higher realms of *kāmaloka* and *rūpaloka*; (2) One becomes a *sotāpanna*, *sakadāgāmi* and *anāgāmi* in *kāmabhūmi*, and an *arahat* in *suddhāvāsa* (five planes).

"Hence the word Bon-sin-san, which means that one goes up the stages of existence one after another.

These two types are obviously different from those mentioned in the Sutta*s*: (1) *sattakkhattuparama sotāpanna* ("One with seven births at the utmost"), (2) *kolankola sotāpanna* ("One passing from one noble family to another"), (3) *ekabīji sotāpanna* ("One germinating only once more").

These three types become *sotāpannas* in *kāmabhūmi* and either in this very existence or later, (not more than seven), become arahats in the same *bhūmi* (sphere)."

See also chapter VIII of this treatise, under "stream-entry." (Editor, The Wheel)

64 It is an individual usage of the author, the Ven. Ledi Sayādaw, to apply the term *sa-upādisesa-nibbāna* also to the *sotāpanna* (and here to the "Bon-sin-san" type). In the canonical and commentarial Pali texts, it is applied only to the arahant who has destroyed all ten fetters (*saṃyojana*), while the *sotāpanna* has abandoned only the first three. This divergent usage may have been caused by the facts that the Sotāpanna is said to have the "first glimpse" (*paṭhama-dassana*) of Nibbāna and that his supramundane path- and fruit-moments have Nibbāna as object (and not conditioned phenomena, as with all mundane consciousness). Hence he can be said to have a first experience of Nibbāna though still imperfect and temporary. (*Editor, The Wheel*).

beings. Having become "Bon-sin-san" *Ariyas* (Noble Ones), they are beings of the *lokuttara* (supramundane sphere).

Here ends the part showing *uppanna-* and *anuppanna-akusala kammas* from which *sotāpannas* have obtained their release.

Arisen and Not-arisen Wholesome Acts *(Uppanna and Anuppanna Kusala Kamma)*

I shall now show the division of *kusala-kammas* into *uppanna* and *anuppanna,* first with reference to the three qualities of *sīla*, *samādhi*, and *paññā*, and second with reference to the seven purifications *(satta visuddhi)*; (see p. 17).

Wrong View *(Diṭṭhi)*

When it is said that *saṃsāra*, the round of rebirths, is very terrifying, it is because of the evil deeds (*duccarita*), arisen (*uppanna*) in the past and present and not-arisen (*anuppanna*); but still to arise in the future, (i.e., potential) which have wrong view as their root. When it is said that there is no hiding place, no haven, on which one can depend, it is because of the selfsame evil deeds and wrong views.

When wrong views are extinguished, both old and new evil deeds (*duccarita*) are also extinguished. When old and new evil deeds are extinguished, release from (rebirth in) the lower worlds (*apāya*; see note 14) is attained and only exalted states of humans, *devas* (celestials) and *brahmās* (higher divinities) remain. Since beings have to cultivate a desire for an encounter with a Buddha Sāsana in order to secure release from rebirth in the lower worlds and from old and new evil deeds, now that they have encountered the Teaching of the Buddha (Buddha Sāsana) in this very existence, it behoves them to make an attempt of extinguishing the great evil of wrong views.

Wrong view is established in beings in three planes or layers, viz:

1, *Vītikkama*, transgression (in deeds or speech)
2. *Pariyuṭṭhāna*, obsession of the mind by evil thoughts; mental involvement with the stains or defilements (*kilesa*)

3. *Anusaya*, proclivity, or latent disposition to the stains[65]

These layers are the realm of *sakkāya-diṭṭhi*. They may be called coarse, middling and fine aspects of wrong view.

I shall now discuss how the results of *diṭṭhi* (wrong view), the ten evil deeds enter into these layers of *diṭṭhi*.

The coarse layer of wrong view, *vītikkama* comprises *akusala-kamma*, committed through overt deeds and speech. The middle layer of *pariyuṭṭhāna* comprises the evils that occur in thoughts. The finest layer, *anusaya*, is the evil that lies latent in the personalities of beings throughout the beginningless round of rebirths (*anamatagga-saṃsāra*), though it may not yet result in manifestations of acts, speech or thoughts.

It may be said that there are three kinds of fire in a match-box. The first is the fire that lies latent in the whole box of matches. The second is the fire that ignites the match stick when it is struck. The third is the fire that is transferred to another object when it is brought in contact with the flame of the match stick. Such a fire is that which burns rubbish heaps, clothes, houses, monasteries, and villages.

This last fire, the fire that is transferred to another object, resembles the coarse *vītikkama-diṭṭhi*, manifested in transgressions by acts and speech. The fire that burns the match stick resembles *pariyuṭṭhāna-diṭṭhi* which is manifested in the mind every time it comes in contact with objects of thought. The fire that is latent in the box of matches resembles the *anusaya-diṭṭhi* that resides in the personalities of beings throughout the succession of lives in *anamatagga-saṃsāra*, the unfathomable aeons of existence.

This fire that lies latent in the box of matches does not burst into flame so long as the match head is not rubbed with the nitrous surface of the match-box. It does not cause any harm even if it be kept in contact with highly inflammable articles such as gunpowder. In the same way, the *anusaya-diṭṭhi* lies latent in the personality and does not manifest itself so long as it does not come into contact with evil objects of thought or other causes of evil. When, however, evil objects of thought or other causes impinge on the six sense-doors, the *anusaya-diṭṭhi* is disturbed and begins to make itself manifest in the mind-door, or in the plane of the *pariyuṭṭhāna* through the function

65 See *Manual of Insight* (*The Wheel* No. 31/32), p. 79ff.

of volition. If at that time the manifestations can be suppressed by good doctrines, they disappear from the *pariyuṭṭhāna* plane and return to the *anusaya* plane and reside there as latent natural tendencies. If they cannot be suppressed, they continue to manifest themselves as developing volitions. If they are further disturbed (in the *pariyuṭṭhāna* plane), they manifest themselves in the *vītikkama* plane in the form of evil speech or evil acts.

In this world, if a person can control himself in the *vītikkama* and *pariyuṭṭhāna* planes, and if thereby his acts, speech, and thoughts are, so to say, clean and unsoiled, he is called a good, pious, or moral man. But such a person is not aware of the *anusaya* plane. If the *anusaya* plane is not destroyed, even if perfect control is exercised over the *vītikkama* and *pariyuṭṭhāna* planes, such control can only be of a temporary nature. If the person is strong in the observance of good principles, the control can last for the whole of this life. But there can be no certainty about the next life, when upheavals in these two planes may recur.

Lobha (greed), *dosa*, and *moha* also have each of them three planes.

In order to destroy these three planes of *diṭṭhi* completely, men have to put forth effort in the three *sikkhās* of *sīla*, *samādhī*, and *paññā*. They have to practice the seven *visuddhis*.

As far as laypeople are concerned, *sīla* means *ājīvaṭṭhamaka-sīla* which is *nicca-sīla* for them. The *aṭṭhāṅga-uposatha-sīla* and *dasaṅga-sīla* add refinement to *nicca-sīla*. It is a good thing to be able to observe them but it does not matter much if they cannot be observed. For those people who assume the yellow garb of *Isis*,[66] the *ājīvaṭṭhamaka-sīla* and *dasaṅga-sīla* constitute *sīla*. The *aṭṭhaṅga-uposatha-sīla* is included in the *dasaṅga-sīla*. For bhikkhus, the *catupārisuddhi-sīla* constitutes morality (*sīla*).[67]

Preliminary, access-, and full *concentration*[68] which are obtained by mindful body contemplation (such as on out-and in-breath) or by meditating on the bones of the body (as one of the thirty-two parts), constitute concentration (*samādhi*).

---

66 Hermits, recluses, rishis.

67 The Pali terms occurring in this para. are explained in notes 20-24.

68 *Apparikamma-*, *upacāra-* and *appanā-samādhi*,—See *Path of Purification* (*Visuddhimagga*), Ch. 11, 25, IV, 32.

The four mundane purifications,[69] together with supramundane purification by knowledge and vision (*lokuttara-ñāṇadassana-visuddhi*)—these constitute wisdom (*paññā*).

Among the three planes of wrong view, morality (*sīla*) destroys the plane of transgression (*vītikama*). This means that if one possesses the purification of morality (*sīla-visuddhi*), upheavals in deeds and speech cannot occur. Concentration (*samādhi*) can destroy wrong view on the plane of mental obsession (*pariyuṭṭhāna*). This means that if attention to meditative practice (*bhāvānā-manasikāra*) is firmly established, upheavals in thought cannot occur. Wisdom (*paññā*) destroys wrong view on the *anusaya* plane of proclivity. This means that, if insight is obtained into the entire personality as a mere grouping of mental and bodily processes (*nāma* and *rūpa*) and as a grouping that is impermanent, painful and without a self, then the latent store of wrong view that may manifest itself in the wrong notions of a person (*puggala*), living being (*satta*), permanency, pleasure and self (*attā*), will disappear. So long as this proclivity to wrong view (*diṭṭhi-anusaya*) exists, the destruction of the plane of transgression by morality and of the plane of mental obsession by concentration, can be no more than temporary.

In the division of acts as "arisen" and "not arisen" (*uppanna, anuppanna*), there are two methods: 1) division based on this life as the starting point, and 2) division based on the past infinite *saṃsāra* as the starting point.

I shall now show the method based on this life as the starting point. In those who have never undertaken to keep moral precepts (*sīla*) in this life, there is no arisen morality (*uppanna-sīla*). In those who at one time or other in this life have undertaken to keep *sīla*, such morality is "arisen." The same applies to concentration and wisdom: what was attained in this life is "arisen," and what was never attained in this life is "not arisen."

In the method based on the past *saṃsāra* as the starting point, there are two kinds of morality, mundane and supramundane (*lokiya* and *lokuttara-sīla*). Mundane morality is "arisen" (*uppanna*), because there is no being who at one time or other in the past *saṃsāra* has not undertaken to keep the rules of mundane morality. But

69 These are the 3rd, 4th, 5th and 6th purifications of the list of the seven *saddhammas* listed on p. 17.

supramundane morality (*lokuttara-sīla*), as far as unliberated worldlings (*puthujjana*) are concerned, is "not arisen" (*anuppanna*).

Concentration (*samādhi*) is also of two kinds, mundane and supramundane. Since mundane concentration had been attained on many occasions by beings in the past *saṃsāra*, it is "arisen." Supramundane concentration in the case of worldlings, is not "arisen."

Wisdom is likewise of these two kinds, mundane and supramundane. The four mundane purifications (*lokiyavisuddhi*; see note 78) are mundane wisdom and are "arisen" (*uppanna*) for those who have encountered Buddha Sāsanas in the past and have practiced these purifications; they are "not arisen" (*anuppanna*) for those who have never encountered any Buddha Sāsana in past *saṃsāra*. The purification by knowledge and vision (*ñāṇadassana-visuddhi*) is supramundane wisdom (*lokuttara-paññā*). As far as worldlings are concerned, it is for them "not arisen" since it was never attained by them in the past *saṃsāra*.

I shall now show the four modes of effort (*padhāna*).

(1) The opportunity of ridding oneself completely of arisen, i.e., old unwholesome *kamma* (*uppanna-akusala-kamma*) obtains only when one encounters a Buddha Sāsana.

(2) The opportunity of preventing the appearance of new unwholesome *kamma* (*anuppanna-akusala-kamma*) in the series of existences that are to follow, is also one that can arise only through encountering a Buddha Sāsana. Even though one's journey through *saṃsāra* be infinitely long, if one does not encounter a Buddha's Teaching, no opportunity of ridding oneself of these two classes of unwholesome *kamma* can arise. This is because the task of ridding oneself of them is identical with the task of destroying the *anusaya* plane of *sakkāya-diṭṭhi* (personality-belief), i.e., the latent disposition for such a wrong view. And the destruction of that *anusaya* plane is the work of *anattā-bhāvanā*, i.e., the meditation on not-self, which appears only at the time of a Buddha Sāsana.

Those beings who are destined to be Solitary Buddhas (*paccekabuddha*) had first acquired the seeds of *anattā-bhāvanā* during their encounter with a Sāsana. When there is no Buddha Sāsana in the world, even the mere sound of *anattā* is not heard. And by "the sound of *anattā*" is meant the sound of such terms which formulate the impersonal nature of existence, as *rupā*, *nāma*, *khandha*, *dhātu*, *āyatana*, and *paṭicca-samuppāda*. The whole of the *Abhidhamma Piṭaka* is replete with the sound of *anattā*; and so is the whole of its compendium, the Abhidhammatthasaṅgaha.[70]

The work of *anattā-bhāvanā* consists, first, of fulfilling purification of morality (*sīla-visuddhi*), then of setting up body contemplation (*kāyagatāsati*), and after tranquilizing and controlling one's madly tempestuous and unstable mind, of putting forth effort in the work of *samatha* and *vipassanā* (tranquillity and insight meditation). It is only when the plane of proclivity to wrong views (*diṭṭhi-anusaya*) is destroyed through such effort that all the wrong views, arisen and not arisen (*uppanna* and *anuppanna-micchā-diṭṭhi*) and the evil deeds (*duccarita*) disappear.

(3) The effort to cause the appearance in one's personality of wholesome actions (*kusala-kamma*) which have not appeared before.

(4) The effort to preserve and maintain in one's personality the wholesome actions that have already appeared, these efforts should be undertaken for a successful completion of *anattā-bhāvanā*, after the establishment of body contemplation.

Arisen and Not-arisen morality *(Uppanna- and Anuppanna-sīla)*

Anuppanna-sīla, i.e., morality which has never occurred in the life of worldlings (*puthujjana*) throughout the past infinite *saṃsāra*, consists of three factors of the supramundane Eightfold Path: right speech, right action and right livelihood. They are comprised in the path of stream-entry (*sotāpatti-magga*) and have Nibbāna as their object. This morality destroys the evil acts manifesting themselves in action, speech and wrong modes of earning a living. From the moment that this destruction has taken place, the evils appearing in those three forms, do not appear again even for an instant throughout the succession of many lives and many world cycles that follow.

This class of supramundane morality is achieved only when *anattā-bhāvanā* is successfully practiced. Beings must attempt to

70 Translated in *A Comprehensive Manual of Abhidhamma*, General Editor: Bhikkhu Bodhi, B.P.S., Kandy).

achieve this *anuppanna-sīla* while yet living at the time of a Buddha Sāsana. This means that from the moment of setting up purification of morality (*sīla-visuddhi*), together with body contemplation (*kāyagatāsati*), up to the successful completion of *anattā-bhāvanā*, beings must attempt without relaxation to practice the thirty-seven *bodhipakkhiya-dhammā*, the requisites of enlightenment.

Uppanna-sīla, which has often occurred in past infinite *saṃsāra*, means mundane morality (*lokiya-sīla*) or sense-sphere morality (*kāmāvacara-sīla*). When it is said that attempts must be made to attain a fixation of that *sīla* (i.e., its firm preservation, being the fourth right effort), it must be understood that there are two planes of mundane morality, viz, *niyāma* (stable, unchangeable) and *aniyāma* (unstable, changeable). The state of an *ariya* (saint) is that of stability (*niyāma*), while the state of a worldling (*puthujjana*) is that of instability.

The mundane morality of the sense-sphere attains to the plane of stability in the personalities of stream-enterers (*sotāpanna*). Saints who are *sotāpannas* do not transgress the *ājīvaṭṭhamaka-sīla* (the eightfold morality ending with right livelihood) even in their dreams throughout the series of lives and world-cycles that follow until the final attainment of Parinibbāna.

In the case of unliberated worldlings (*puthujjana*), however, the mundane morality of the sense-sphere is still on the plane of instability (*aniyāma*). These persons have been virtuous lay individuals on an infinite number of occasions in the past. They have also suffered in the lower worlds of misery (*apāya-loka*) countless numbers of times. They have been virtuous hermits and bhikkhus on other infinite occasions. In all their past existences however, they have never been free from the danger of being liable to rebirth in the lower worlds of misery. Even now, the number of beings in these lower worlds is countless, and so is the number of humans, *devas* and *Brahmas* who are on the brink of being born in the lower worlds of misery.

Hence, those beings who possess mundane morality of the sense sphere (*kāmāvacara-lokiya-sīla*) which is still unstable (*aniyāma*), and which, so to say, resides in them for just a temporary short moment, should attempt, while there is yet opportunity within a Buddha

Sāsana, to transform it into the plane of stability (*niyāma*). They should set up body contemplation, and having done so, should practice the *bodhipakkhiya-dhammas* until the function of *anattābhāvanā* is successfully completed.

Arisen and Not-Arisen Concentration *(Uppanna and Anuppanna samādhi)*

Concentration (*samādhi*) as well as wisdom (*paññā*); have likewise two planes, i.e., stability (*niyāma*) and instability (*aniyāma*).

The full concentration of the *jhānas* (*appanā-samādhi*), which is identical with the eight or nine meditative attainments (*samāpatti*),[71] becomes "stable" only on attainment of the stage of a non-returner (*anāgāmi*). The wisdom (*paññā*) that carries the *tādi* quality (of equability)[72] becomes "stable" only at the stage of an arahat.

I shall now describe the concentration and wisdom that *sotāpannas* (stream-winners) achieve.

In accordance with the Cūla-Vedalla Sutta,[73] right effort, right mindfulness and right concentration which are comprised within *sotāpatti-magga* (path of stream-entry), having Nibbāna as object, are called supramundane concentration (*lokuttara-samādhi*).

These three constituents of the *samādhi* group (within the supramundane Eightfold Path) can extinguish once and for all, through overcoming by eradication (*samuccheda-pahāna*),[74],the mental evils of covetousness (*abhijjhā*) and ill will (*vyāpāda*) which have *micchā-vāyāma* (wrong effort), *micchā-sati* (wrong attention) and

71 The eight meditative attainments (*attha-samāpatti*) are the four meditative absorptions of the form sphere (*rūpajjhāna*) and the four of the formless sphere (*arūpajjhāna*). The nine attainments are these eight and *nirodha-samāpatti*, the temporary suspension of conscious mental activity.

72 *Tādi* (lit:. such-like, the same) is an equanimous state of mind that cannot be influenced by the ups and downs of life. It is also a designation of the Buddha and the arahat.

73 *Yā ca visākha sammā-vāyamā yā ca sammā-sati yo ca sammā-samādhi, ime dhammā samādhikkhandhe saṅgahitā*: "And whatever there is of right effort, right mindfulness and right concentration, these things are comprised in the category of concentration" (MN 44).

74 See *Manual of Insight* (*The Wheel* No. 31/32), p. 79f.

micchā-samādhi (wrong concentration) as their roots. From the instance they are eradicated, those mental evils of covetousness and ill will do not arise again throughout the many lives and world-cycles that may follow. It is the kind of concentration that can be achieved only within a Buddha Sāsana, when meditative cultivation of the *anattā* doctrine (*anattā-bhāvanā*) appears. Hence, now that beings have encountered a Buddha Sāsana, they should endeavour to achieve that so far not-arisen kind of concentration (*anuppanna-samādhi*), before they become severed from the Sāsana by the vicissitudes of wandering in *saṃsāra*. This means, that, beginning with body contemplation, they should practice the *bodhipakkhiya-dhammas* until they attain the successful culmination of *anattā-bhāvanā.*

Uppanna-samādhi, which has occurred a countless number of times in infinite past *saṃsāra*, consists of concentration of the sense-sphere (*kāmāvacara-samādhi*), i.e., neighborhood concentration), of the fine-material (*rūpāvacaras*) and immaterial sphere (*arūpāvacaras*). When it was said that attempts must be made for the "stability" (*niyāma*) of arisen concentration it must be understood that this mundane concentration has likewise two planes, viz. stability and instability. The mundane right effort, right mindfulness and right concentration, with which *ariyas* (noble ones) are endowed, are on the plane of "stability" (*niyāma*). The evil deeds (*duccarita*) of covetousness and ill will do not arise in them even in dreams throughout the succession of lives and world-cycles that follow until the final attainment of Parinibbāna.

The triple (path-) group of mundane concentration with which worldlings are endowed, is on the plane of "instability" (*aniyāma*). In the infinite past *saṃsāra*, these persons have been men of *samādhi*, hermits (*isis*) of *samādhi*, and bhikkhus of *samādhi* endowed with *jhānas* and supernormal powers (*iddhi*), during countless existences. In the life-period of every world-system, there are four world-cycles (*kappa*), each of unfathomable duration. In three of these world-cycles, these worldlings have been *brahmās* in the *brahma* worlds. In every one of these world-systems there have also appeared *apāya*-worlds of misery. And these worlds of misery have been filled by these self-same *Brahmā* Gods, hungry ghosts (*peta*), beings of hell, animals and Titans (*asura*). Compared with the infinitely long *samsāra*, the period of each of these world-systems is just like that of an eye-wink.

Thus it behoves us all to attempt the transformation of the instability of the three constituents of the *samādhi* group (which we temporarily acquired in the past on many occasions) to the stage of stability (*niyāma*), while we still have the opportunity now in the midst of an age in which the Buddha Sāsana exists. Hence we should, after first setting up body contemplation, practice the *bodhipakkhiya-dhammas* until successful completion of *anattā-bhāvanā.*

Arisen and Not-arisen Wisdom *(Uppanna and Anuppanna-paññā)*

In accordance with the Cūla-Vedalla Sutta, right understanding and right thought, which are comprised in *sotāpattimagga* and have Nibbāna as their object, are called supramundane wisdom. This wisdom destroys the *anusaya* plane of *sakkāya-diṭṭhi* completely, and dispels, by way of an eradicating abandonment (*samuccheda-pahāna*), every vestige of wrong understanding and wrong thought, together with the evil deeds (*duccarita*) and wrong livelihood (*durājīva*), once and for all. The old store accumulated by past evil *kamma* also disappears completely. Release is obtained from the *apāya-saṃsāra*, i.e., rebirth in the lower worlds of misery. From this instant the evils of wrong views and evil deeds do not make an appearance throughout the series of future existence and future world-cycles.

This kind of wisdom appears only during a Buddha Sāsana when *anattā-bhāvanā* exists. Hence, as beings have now encountered a Buddha Sāsana, they should endeavour to attain this *anuppanna-paññā*, a wisdom so far not arisen to them, before they are bereft of this Sāsana (in future lives). This means that, starting with body contemplation, they should practice the *bodhipakkhiya-dhammā* until they reach the successful culmination of *anattā-bhāvanā*.

Those kinds of wisdom that have often appeared (*uppanna*) in the past infinite *saṃsāra* are: the right understanding that beings are owners of (or responsible for) their actions (*kammassakatā-sammā-diṭṭhi*); all kinds of (mundane) knowledge and wisdom on the level of the sense-sphere (*kāmāvacara*), and such supernormal knowledges (*abhiññā*) as the celestial eye (*dibba-cakkhu*) and the celestial ear (*dibba-sota*) (i.e., clairvoyance and clairaudience).

When it was said that attempts must be made for the "stability" (*niyāma*) of wisdom, it must be understood that this mundane wisdom has likewise two planes, viz. stability and instability. The mundane right understanding and right thoughts of *ariyas* (noble ones) are established on the plane of stability (*niyāma*). From the moment they are thus established in that stable wisdom, and throughout the series of lives that follow until they attain Parinibbāna, they will always be in the possession of the right understanding of ownership of *kamma* (*kammassakatā-sammā-diṭṭhi*), of doctrinal knowledge (*pariyatti-ñāṇa*), knowledge of *dhamma*-practice (*paṭipatti-ñāṇa*), and knowledge of the four truths (*catu-sacca-ñāṇa*).

The twofold mundane wisdom, however, with which worldlings (*puthujjana*) are endowed, is on the plane of instability (*aniyāma*). In their wanderings through *saṃsāra*, these worldlings have sometimes been learned in the Dhamma, sometimes acquired fame through their learning, sometimes they were great monks or great physicians, while at other times they have also been cockles, snails, worms, leeches, lice, bugs, maggots, ticks etc.—creatures that could be said to be just alive.

Hence, while now the opportunity of an encounter with a Buddha Sāsana offers itself, efforts must be made to transform unstable wisdom (which is but a temporary acquisition) into stable wisdom, in the way stated above.

This ends the detailed exposition of the two types of morality, concentration and wisdom, viz. as arisen and not-arisen.

With this background, those laymen, hermits and bhikkhus who have encountered a Buddha Sāsana in this life, who desire to rid themselves of evils in their future existences, and who wish to consolidate in themselves permanently such *dhammas* as purification of virtue, etc., should practice appropriately the foundations of mindfulness (*satipaṭṭhāna*), applying energy of the type of the right efforts (*sammāpadhāna*), in order to destroy the *anusaya* plane of personality belief.

If they desire to free themselves from the insane and wild mind such as is possessed by the madman, the incapable boatman, the man afflicted with hydrophobia, and the sick man who vomits his medicines (as described in Chapter II), and desire to consolidate their concentration or transform it to a stable condition (*niyāma*), so as to enable them to keep their attention tranquil, steady and fixed at will on any subject of meditation (*kammaṭṭhāṇa*), they should practice appropriately the foundations of mindfulness, with *sammāpadhāna* energy in order to destroy thereby the *anusaya* plane of personality belief.

If they desire to free themselves from doctrines and conditions of delusion (*sammoha-dhamma*) which can cast them into the utter darkness of the absence of wisdom; which can extirpate all feelings of respect and reverence that they have harboured towards the infinite and noble qualities of the Buddha, the Dhamma and the *Ariya* Sangha, as also of the establishments of the Sāsana, leaving no trace in the existences that follow; if they desire to rid themselves of the great wrong doctrines (*micchādhamma*) that have led them in the past beginningless *saṃsāra* to approach, respect and pay reverence to all manners of spurious Buddhas (or religious teachers), because as worldlings they were not in a position to know the true Buddha, the true Dhamma and the true Sangha; if they desire to attain, in the series of existences and world-cycles beginning with the present, that faith known as firmly established faith, (*adhigama-saddhā*) and that wisdom known as firmly established wisdom (*adhigama-paññā*), by virtue of which they can continue to evoke within themselves, without let or hindrance, respect and reverence for the true Buddha, the true Dhamma and the true Sangha; and if they desire to transform them to the level of "stability" (*niyāma*), then they must practice appropriately the foundations of mindfulness, with *sammāpadhāna* effort, with a view of destroying personality belief on its plane of latent dispositions (*anusaya-bhūmi*). Here, the appropriate practice of right effort (*sammāpadhāna*) means that energy which is accompanied by the determination, "Let the skin remain; let the bones remain…, etc."

CHAPTER IV

The Bases of Success *(Iddhipāda)*

I shall now give a brief description of the *iddhipādas*, the bases of success.

Iddhi

The word-explanation is: "*ijjhanam iddhi*"; this means the fact of having succeeded, completed or perfected.[75]

In the Buddha Sāsana there are five *iddhis*:

1. *Abhiññeyyesu dhammesu abhiññā-siddhi*[76]
2. *Pariññeyyesu dhammesu pariññā-siddhi*
3. *Pahātabbesu dhammesu pahāna-siddhi*
4. *Sacchikātabbesu dhammesu sacchikiriya-siddhi*
5. *Bhāvetabbesu dhammesu bhāvanā-siddhi*

1. Completion of or success in acquiring special knowledge regarding those things in which special knowledge should be acquired, things such as *rūpa* (material phenomena), *nāma* (mental phenomena);

2. Completion of or success in acquiring full understanding in those things regarding which full understanding should be acquired, things such as *dukkha sacca* (the Noble Truth of Suffering);

---

75 See *The Path of Purification* (*Visuddhimagga*), tr. by Ñāṇamoli Thera Ch. XII, § 20-22, 44. As will be seen from this chapter the terms *iddhi* and *iddhipāda* do not exclusively refer to supernormal (magical) powers, as it is sometimes assumed. In the present context, they signify success in Dhamma-practice and the four basic conditions of such success. Also, in the first part of this chapter, the translator's rendering of *iddhi* by "completion" has been retained while, elsewhere the preferable translation by "success" has been used (Editor).

76 *Siddhi* is identical with *iddhi*.

3. Completion of or success attained in the task of abandonment of those things that should be abandoned, things such as *samudaya-sacca* (the Noble Truth of the Cause of Suffering);

4. Completion of or success attained in the task of realization of those things that should be realized, things such as *nirodha-sacca* (the Noble Truth of the Cessation of Suffering);

5. Completion of or success attained in the task of development or cultivation of those things that should be developed or cultivated, things such as *magga-sacca* (the Noble Truth of the Path leading to the Cessation of Suffering).

These are the five essential *iddhis* within a Buddha Sāsana.

Abhiññā-siddhi means the completion of the task of knowing of the *paramattha-dhammas* (ultimate truths) which one had no knowledge of while one was beyond the pale of a Buddha Sāsana. A thorough knowledge of the *Abhidhammattha-saṅgaha* (a summary of all the essential doctrines of the Abhidhamma[77]) amounts to *abhiññā-siddhi.*

Pariññā-siddhi means the completion of acquiring full understanding of *dukkha sacca* (the Noble Truth of Suffering) either through a knowledge of their *lakkhaṇa* (characteristics), *rasa* (functions), *paccupaṭṭhāna* (manifestations), and *padaṭṭhāna* (proximate causes), or through a knowledge of the three characteristics of impermanence, *dukkha*, and *anattā*, which they possess.

Pahāna-siddhi means the completion of the task of abandoning (*pahāna*), i.e., destroying the *kilesas* (defilements) which are *samudaya sacca* (the Noble Truth of the Cause of Suffering). In this book, since the main emphasis is placed on the attainment of the lowest class of *sotāpannas*, namely the "bon-sin-san" *sotāpannas*, and not on the higher classes of *ariyas* (noble ones), the completion of the task of destroying *sakkāya-diṭṭhi* is *pahāna-siddhi.* The task of dispelling *vicikicchā* (sceptical doubt) is comprised within the task of destroying *sakkāya-diṭṭhi*.

Sacchikiriya-siddhi means: the completion of the task of realizing *nirodha sacca* (the Noble Truth of the Cessation of Suffering) both bodily and mentally. This task consists of the suppression and destruction of the *kilesas* (defilements).

77 See note 79.

Bhāvanā-siddhi means: the development of the three *sikkhās* of *sīla* (morality), *samādhi* (mental concentration) and *paññā* (wisdom), until the attainment of *lokuttara magga sacca* (supramundane path leading to the cessation of suffering).

Also the seven purifications, beginning with morality, and their sub-divisions, constitute as many kinds of *iddhi*, in the sense of potencies in their respective fields.

Iddhipāda

The word-explanation is: *iddhiyā pādo iddhipādo*, i.e., root or basis of attaining completion or perfection (success or potency).[78]

There are four kinds of *iddhipādas*. They are:

1. *Chandiddhipāda* (*chanda*)
2. *Viriyiddhipāda* (*viriya*)
3. *Cittiddhipādo* (*citta*)
4. *Vimaṃsiddhipāda* (*vimaṃsa* or *paññā*)

By *chanda* is meant (the zeal or) desire to obtain, desire to attain, desire to reach, desire to fulfil, desire to accomplish. The desire indicated here is extreme or excessive desire. There is nothing within or without one's personality that can obstruct that desire. It is the kind of desire that evokes the thought, "If I do not attain this accomplishment in this life, I shall not rest content. It is better that I die rather than that I shall not attain it."

It is the kind of desire nurtured by King Dhammasoṇḍa[79] of Benares during the time of the Kassapa Buddha,[80] when the king said to himself, "What use is there in my being king of Benares if I do not get the opportunity of hearing a discourse of the Kassapa Buddha?" The king, therefore, relinquished his throne and went out in search of one who could repeat to him a discourse of the Kassapa Buddha, no matter that the discourse consisted of a short stanza only.

---

78 See *The Path of Purification*, ch.XII, 50-53; XXII, 63.

79 *Rāsavāhinī* (Jambudipuppatti-kathā).

80 A Buddha of a former age.

Such desire is appeased if it is fulfilled, as in the case of King Bimbisāra[81], Visākhā, and Anāthapiṇḍika.[82] It is only when there are faint indications that the desire can be attained but is not fulfilled, that the mind becomes troubled, and thoughts arise that it is better to die than live without attaining the desire.

Examples of such desire existed also in King Temiya,[83] King Hatthipāla,[84] and kings, nobles, and rich men in the time of the Buddha who discarded their palaces, retinues and other luxuries to live the lives of bhikkhus in the Buddha Sāsana.

Viriya means *sammāpadhāna-viriya* together with its four characteristics (see Chapter II). A person with this *viriya* is infused with the thought that the aim can be attained by energy and effort. He is not discouraged even though it is said to him that he must undergo great hardships. He is not discouraged even though he actually has to undergo great hardships. He is not discouraged even though it is said to him that he must put forth effort for many days, months, and years. He is not discouraged even though he actually has to put forth effort for such long periods.

Those who are weak in energy recoil from their task when confronted with work requiring great energy and effort. They shrink when told that they will have to stay apart from friends and associates. They shrink from the prospect of the necessity to be frugal in sleep and food. They shrink from the prospect of long periods of concentration.

Citta (lit.: consciousness) means: attachment to *iddhis* when one comes in contact with the Sāsana and hears the Dhamma. It is attachment that is extremely ardent and strong.

Although one lives amidst the beauties and luxuries of the world, amidst acquired powers and fortunes, amidst the sacred books and the study of them, one is not allured, but one's mind is always turned towards the *iddhis*. One attains satisfaction and tranquillity only when one's mind is absorbed in matters connected with the *iddhis*. It is like the absorption of the alchemist engaged in the

81 See Comy. to Tirokuḍḍa Sutta, in Minor Readings (Khuddakapāṭha), tr. by Ñāṇamoli Thera (PTS), p. 230ff.

82 See Dhammapada Comy., story relating to verse 1.

83 Mūgapakkha Jātaka.

84 Hatthipāla Jātaka.

transmutation of the baser metals into gold or silver. Such an alchemist has no interest in anything else but his alchemy. He forgets to sleep or eat, or whether he had slept or eaten. He does not notice anything when out walking. *Citta* is great absorption or attachment of this nature.

Vimaṃsā (investigation) means: knowledge or wisdom that can clearly perceive the greatness of the sufferings of hell, and of the sufferings attendant on the round of rebirths. It is knowledge that can clearly perceive the advantages and benefits of the *iddhis*. It is knowledge that can dwell on the deep and difficult *dhammas*, and on their nature. A person who possesses such knowledge can no longer find pleasure in any worldly pursuit except the pursuit of the *iddhis*. He finds gratification only in the acquisition of deep and profound *iddhis*. The deeper and more profound the *dhammas*, the greater is his desire to attain them.

Those who are endowed with any one of these four bases of success (*iddhipāda*) can no longer, during this life, admit or plead inability and remain without putting forth effort in the establishment of body contemplation (*kāyagatāsati*) and the higher stages of the Sāsana such as the seven purifications (*visuddhi*). It is only those who have never possessed any one of these bases of success, and who cannot differentiate between the shallowness and profoundness of life, between superficiality and depth of the *dhamma*, who admit or plead inability and remain without making any endeavour.

A person endowed with any one of these four *iddhipādas* can attain, according to his *pāramī*, the *iddhis* until he reaches *lokuttara* (supramundane) *iddhi*, either in this life or as a *deva* in the next life. The cases of those endowed with two, or three, or four *iddhipādas* need no lengthy explanation.

In the cases of those persons who (far from possessing any of the *iddhis*) do not even possess any of the *iddhipādas*, they should attempt to acquire one or other of these bases. They admit or plead inability only because they have not the desire to acquire the higher benefits of the Sāsana, such as the *satipaṭṭhānas*. They should regard this very admission of inability as a highway to the lower worlds of misery (*āpayaloka*). Thus, they should study, think and ponder over the Suttanta discourses that can arouse zeal. They should approach a teacher who can arouse zeal and rely on him.

Hence did the Buddha say:

Chandiddhipādaṃ bhāveti, viriyiddhipādaṃ bhāveti, Cittiddhipādaṃ bhāveti, vimaṃsiddhipādaṃ bhāveti.

He cultivates zeal, energy, consciousness and investigation as the bases of success.

Some persons, far from attaining the *iddhis*, do not even try to attain the *iddhipādas*. If they do not possess *chanda*, they do not even know that it is necessary to acquire such zeal. They are persons who admit and plead inability and defeat. The same is true in the cases of *viriya*, *citta*, and *vimaṃsa*.

Steady application of the mind to *kāyagatāsati*, studying the anecdotes conveying a sense of urgency (*saṃvega*)[85], applying oneself to the strict ascetic observances (*dhutaṅga*) and such other practices of the Dhamma, is setting up of energy (*viriya*). Applying oneself to profound subjects of Dhamma, such as the four great primaries, amounts to the setting up of *vīmaṃsa* (investigation).

If any one of the four bases of success is established, then it is certain that the respective *iddhis*[86] will be attained according to one's *pārami*. Hence, it is stated in the commentaries that persons who do not possess any of the bases of success, resemble the sons of a *caṇḍāla* (an outcaste), while persons possessing one of the bases of success resemble the sons of an emperor. The sons of a *caṇḍāla* never even aim at becoming an emperor because they have no basis, no *pāda*, for such an attainment. Sons of emperors, however, always aim at becoming emperors because they are endowed with the bases for attaining such an aim.

Hence, wise persons of the present day should attempt to acquire the four *iddhipādas*, the bases of success, so that they can destroy the great realm of personality belief and acquire, within the Sāsana, the benefits of the higher attainments that can be obtained according to one's *pāramis*.

---

85 *Saṃvega* is a stirring up of the mind, caused by contemplating the dangers and miseries of *saṃsāra*.

86 That is, one of the five *iddhi* or *siddhis*, mentioned at the beginning of this chapter.

CHAPTER V

THE FIVE CONTROLLING FACULTIES *(Indriya)*

The word-explanation of the term *indriya* is: "*indassa kammaṃ indriyaṃ.*" This means the act of ruling, or of controlling, by rulers. "The act of ruling by rulers" means that wherever the ruler rules, nobody can go against him.

In the present context, the control or rule that one exercises over one's mind is the essential point in these controlling faculties.

These are the five faculties:[87]

1. *Saddhindriya*: faith and confidence
2. *Viriyindriya*: energy
3. *Satindriya*: mindfulness
4. *Samādhindriya*: concentration
5. *Paññindriya*: wisdom

Faith

Saddhindriya is to some extent synonymous with *saddhā*. But there are two kinds of *saddhā*, namely:

1. *Pakati-saddhā*, ordinary faith
2. *Bhāvanā saddhā*, faith developed (or matured) by meditation

The faith and confidence (*saddhā*) that leads ordinary men and women to perform acts of almsgiving (*dāna*), morality (*sīla*) and "surrogate" (or rudimentary) meditation (*bhāvanā*),[88]—is called

87 On the five faculties see *The Way of Wisdom*, by Edward Conze (*The Wheel* No. 65/66).

88 "Surrogate" meditation. The original text of the translation has here "imitation" *bhāvanā*, which sounds more deprecatory than the author may have intended in this context. What is probably meant is a kind of

ordinary faith (*pakati-saddhā*). Here, as was shown in the simile of the madman (Chapter II), although such *saddhā* is to some extent a controlling faculty, its control does not extend to the capacity of controlling the unstable minds of ordinary folk in the work of meditation (*bhāvanā*). Control is exercised over the instability only to the extent of leading to acts of almsgiving, morality and rudimentary meditation.

Without faith and confidence, the mind never inclines to *kusala-kamma* (wholesome volitional actions), for ordinarily it takes delight only in evil acts. This holds true also for the effort to attain to the purification of virtue (*sīla-visuddhi*) or to engage in the study of the sacred texts. This is how ordinary wholesome acts (*pakati-kusala-kamma*) are produced by the control of ordinary faith which is undeveloped by genuine meditation (*abhāvita*).

In the work of attending to a subject of meditation (*kammaṭṭhāna*) for the practice of tranquility and insight, ordinary faith has not sufficient control over the mind as the mind is apt to recoil and rebound from that faith and to turn elsewhere. In meditative work, ordinary faith is not sufficient.

It is developed faith that prepares the seed-bed, so to say, for the acquisition of great strength and power through the practice of meditation, such as mindfulness of breathing.

In the context of the "requisites of enlightenment" it is developed faith that is called *saddhindriya*, the controlling faculty of faith. In the field of meditative exercises, it represents the disappearance of unstable and oscillating attention and the appearance of a clear and steady mind.[89] The mind's attention can be steadily fixed only on those objects which it finds clear and unbefogged. The

---

very rudimentary meditation or contemplation that is not much more than a devotional or pensive mood maintained for some time, which, being of a discursive nature does not reach, by itself, any marked degree of concentration. Being, in this context, one of the three "items of merit making" (*puññā kiriya-vatthu*), it is nevertheless a beneficial practice that may well lead to concentration and meditation proper. (Editor).

89 The aspect of *saddhā* that is especially active here, is confidence, i.e., confidence in the method (and the Dhamma in general) and self-confidence. (Editor).

practice of body contemplation such as mindfulness of breathing, is the preparation of the seed-bed for *bhāvanā-saddhā*, i.e., faith and confidence developed and matured by meditation. If the mind is fixed on the contemplation of the body, such as the out and in-breaths, it amounts to the attainment of developed faith. If then the work is continued in the field of tranquillity and insight the ability to destroy the three planes of personality belief can be acquired even within this life. The work of *samatha* and *vipassanā* needs for their proper performance, reliance on a teacher who is very learned in the Dhamma.

Energy

Viriyindriya is to some extent synonymous with *viriya*. But there are two kinds, or degrees, of *viriya*, namely:

1. *Pakati-viriya*, ordinary energy
2. *Bhāvanā-viriya*, energy developed by meditation.

Another classification is:

1. *Kāyika-viriya*, bodily energy
2. *Cetasika-viriya*, mental energy

Ordinary energy (*pakati-viriya*) can be easily recognized. Persons who possess much ordinary energy in worldly matters can easily attain developed energy (*bhāvanā-viriya*). The strict observances (*dhutaṅga*) of a monk are instances of bodily energy of a developed nature (*kāyika-bhāvanā-viriya*).

If, after setting up developed bodily energy (such as reducing sleep and being alert and energetic), there is still no mental energy (*cetasika-viriya*), such as enthusiasm in keen attention to meditation (*bhāvanā-manasikāra*), then steady application to or concentration on the subjects of meditation (*kammaṭṭhāna*), such as mindfulness of breathing, cannot be attained, and the period of work is unduly lengthened without achieving clarity of mind and perception.

Any kind of work will be properly and appropriately done only if the person performing it obtains quick mastery over it. It will be improperly done if the work obtains mastery over the person. By "the work obtaining mastery over the person" is meant that the work is done without real energy, as a result of which no concrete results appear, and as days and months drag on, distaste for meditation, and slackness in body postures appear, leading to sloth. With the appearance of sloth, progress in the work slows down, and with the slowing down of progress, further sloth develops. The idea then appears that it would be better to change the form of the work. Thus constant changes in forms of work occur, and in that way the work obtains mastery over the person lacking energy.

In meditative work, quick success is obtained only by one endowed with both bodily and mental energy. From the moment when body contemplation is set up, the energy that develops day by day is *bhāvanā-viriya*, energy developed by meditation, and it is this energy that, in the *bodhipakkhiya-dhammas*, is called the faculty of energy, *viriyindriya*. It represents the disappearance of sloth and laziness in meditative work and the appearance of enthusiasm and vigor. The mind takes delight in dwelling on objects on which its attention is strong. Thence, the task of setting up developed energy, and graded development, is identical with that of the faculty of faith (*saddhindriya*).

The faculty of mindfulness (*satindriya*), in the context of the *bodhipakkhiya-dhammas*, means the setting up of mindful body-contemplation (*kāyagatāsati*), e.g., on out and in-breath, and the development of *bhāvanā-sati* (meditative mindfulness), called *satipaṭṭhāna*, until supramundane right mindfulness (*lokuttara-sammā-sati*), as a supramundane path-factor, is reached.

The faculties of concentration and wisdom (*samādhindriya* and *paññindriya*) may be defined and described similarly.

The faculty of concentration dispels the distraction of mind when it is applied in the work of *satipaṭṭhāna* on such an object as the mindfulness on breathing. The faculty of wisdom dispels confusion and haziness.

The faculties of faith, energy and mindfulness, which precede those of concentration and wisdom, are like those who raise a king to kingship. They raise the latter two faculties until the topmost excellence is attained.

After the setting up of body contemplation and the attainment of mastery over one's mind, if the *samatha* road is taken, the faculty of concentration becomes the eight meditative attainments (*samāpatti* or *jhāna*), while the faculty of wisdom becomes the five higher spiritual knowledges (*abhiññā*),[90] such as the supernormal powers etc. If the *vipassanā* road be taken, the faculty of concentration becomes the voidness concentration (*suññatā-samādhi*), conditionless concentration (*animitta-samādhi*), or desireless concentration (*appaṇihita-samādhi*), while the faculty of wisdom becomes the five purifications (*visuddhi*) pertaining to wisdom,[91] the knowledge of the three contemplations (*anupassanā-ñāṇa*),[92] the ten insight knowledges (*vipassanā-ñāṇa*),[93] the knowledges pertaining to the four paths and the four fruitions and the nineteen of reviewing (*paccavekkhaṇa-ñāṇa*).[94]

This shows how the five faculties occur together.

The Predominance of the Faculties

It is now proposed to show where each of these faculties forms a predominant factor.

The Sutta text says:

> *Kattha saddhindriyaṃ daṭṭhabbaṃ? Catūsu sotā pattiyaṅgesu ettha saddhindriyaṃ daṭṭhabbaṃ.*
>
> Where should one look for the faculty of faith? One should look for it in four constituents of stream-entry.[95]

---

90 The five higher spiritual knowledges (*abhiññā*) are 1) *iddhividha* (supernormal powers), 2) *dibba-sota*: (celestial clairaudience), 3) *parassa cetopariyañāṇa* (knowledge of the minds of others), 4) *pubbe nivāsānussati* (recollection of former lives), and 5) *dibba-cakkhu* (clairvoyance).

91 These are the last five of the seven purifications: see list in the Introduction.

92 These are the contemplations on impermanence, suffering and not-self.

93 These are: comprehension knowledge (*sammasana-ñāṇa*), and the nine insight-knowledges dealt with in Chapter XXI of The Path of Purification.

94 These nineteen are enumerated in *The Path of Purification*, XXII, 20, 21.

95 *Sotannassa angāni*; see Indriya Saṃyutta, Sutta 8, Daṭṭhabba Sutta.

This means that the faculty of faith predominates in the four constituents of stream-entry. These four are:

1. Unshakable faith in the noble qualities of the Buddha, such as *arahaṃ*, *sammā-sambuddho*, etc.
2. Unshakable faith in the noble qualities of the Dhamma, such as "well proclaimed" (*svākkhāto*), etc.
3. Unshakable faith in the noble qualities of the Sangha, such as "of good conduct" (*supaṭipanno*), etc.
4. Completely or perfectly endowed with the foundation (or proximate cause: *padaṭṭhāna*) of supramundane concentration (*lokuttara-samādhi*), which is purification of morality (*sīla-visuddhi*)[96]

These are the four factors that ensure the attainment of *sotāpatti-magga-ñāṇa* (knowledge pertaining to the path of stream-entry) within the compass of this life.

In the sutta passage[97] "*Buddhe aveccappasādena samannāgato*", *aveccappasādo* means "unshakable faith." It is the faith (*saddhā*) of those who have attained access concentration (*upacāra-samādhi*) while reflecting on the noble qualities of the Buddha. *Upacāra-samādhi* here means steady and fixed attention achieved while reflecting on the noble qualities of the Buddha. When one encounters such steady and fixed attention, one must know that the control by faith is predominant. Such a person is one who attains mastery over his mind in the matter of faith in the noble qualities of the Buddha. The same holds true in regard to the noble qualities of the Dhamma and Sangha.

"Foundation of supramundane concentration" (the fourth constituent of stream-entry) means the "permanent morality ending with right livelihood as the eighth precept" (*ājīvaṭṭhamaka-nicca-sīla*) which can enable one to attain supramundane concentration in this very life. When that *sīla* is unbroken and pure, it is free from the defilements of *taṇhā*, *māna* (conceit), and *diṭṭhi* (wrong view), and in such case one must understand that *saddhā* is prominent in that

96 In the sutta*s*, this fourth constituent of stream-entry is usually formulated as "unbroken morality".

97 For instance, in Majjhima Nikāya Sutta 9, translated in The Discourse on Right View (Sammādiṭṭhi Sutta, The Wheel no. 377/379).

sīla. Inability to observe the requirements of the *sīla* is called "breaking" it. Although the *sīla* may be technically unbroken, if it is observed amidst ordinary worldly conditions, it is said to be "impure". In accordance with the saying "the worth of a bull can be known only on the ascent from the bed of a stream to the banks," lay-persons and bhikkhus who profess to be followers of the Buddha can know whether or not the turbulence and distractions latent in their minds have disappeared, (i.e., whether or not they have obtained mastery over their minds) only when they arrive at these four constituents.

Kattha viriyindriyaṃ daṭṭhabbaṃ?
Catūsu sammpadhānesu ettha vīriyindriyaṃ daṭṭhabbaṃ.

Where should one look for the faculty of energy?
One should look for it in the four constituents of right effort.

Lay persons and bhikkhus who profess to be followers of the Buddha can know whether or not the unsettledness and turbulence of their minds in the matter of *viriya* have disappeared and whether or not they are thus persons who have obtained mastery over their minds, only when they come to the four constituents of *sammappadhāna* (right effort).

"Let my skin remain, let my sinews remain, let my bones remain, let my blood dry up, I shall not rest until the realm of personality belief (*sakkāya-diṭṭhi*), the realm of the *duccaritas*, and the *apāya-saṃsāra*, that are in my personality, are destroyed in this life." This is the singleness of determination and effort in *sammāpadhāna*. It is the effort of the same order as that exerted by the Venerable Cakkhupāla's.[98] When one encounters such determination and effort, one must recognise in it the predominating control of *viriya* over the mind. In the matter of *viriya*, the unsettledness and turbulence of the mind have disappeared in such a person, and he is one within the Buddha Sāsana who has obtained mastery over his mind.

Kattha satindriyaṃ daṭṭhabbaṃ?
Catūsu satipaṭṭhānesu ettha satiṅdriyaṃ daṭṭhabbaṃ.

---

98 See Dhammapada Comy., story to verse 1.

Where should one look for the faculty of mindfulness? One should look for it in the four foundations of mindfulness.

Lay persons and bhikkhus who profess to be followers of the Buddha can know whether or not the unsettledness and turbulence of their minds in the matter of *sati* (mindfulness) have disappeared, and whether or not they are thus persons who have obtained mastery over their minds, only when they arrive at the four constituents of the *satipaṭṭhāna*. If the attention can be kept fixed on any part of the body, such as out-breath and in-breath, by the successful practice of mindful body contemplation (*kāyagatāsati*) for as long as is desired, then it must be recognized as the control exercised by mindfulness (*sati*). The unsettledness and turbulence of the mind of such a person have disappeared. He is one who has obtained mastery over his mind.

Kattha samādhindriyaṃ daṭṭhabbaṃ?
Catūsu jhānesu ettha samādhindriyaṃ daṭṭhabbaṃ.

Where should one look for the faculty of concentration? One should look for it in the four *jhānas*.

If in the work of *samatha* (such as out-breath and in-breath) at least the successful accomplishment of *upacāra-samādhi-bhāvanā* (contemplation of access-concentration) is attained, and if thereby the *nīvaraṇas* (hindrances) such as *kāmacchanda* (sensuous desire), *vyāpāda* (ill will), which in the past *saṃsāra* have continuously been running riot in the mind, are removed, the attention of the mind on the objects of *samatha* becomes specially steady and tranquil. This should be recognized as arising out of the function of the predominant control exercised by *samādhi*. The unsettledness and disturbances of the mind in the matter of *samādhi* have disappeared from such an individual. He is one who has obtained mastery over his mind.

Kattha paññindriyaṃ daṭṭhabbaṃ?
Catūsu ariyasaccesu ettha paññindriyaṃ daṭṭhabbaṃ.

Where should one look for the faculty of wisdom? One should look for it in the Four Noble Truths.

Among persons who encounter a Buddha Sāsana, knowledge of the Four Noble Truths is of supreme value. Only when this knowledge is acquired can they obtain release from the realm of *sakkāya-diṭṭhi*, and that of the *duccaritas*, and from the *āpaya-saṃsāra*. Hence, in order to acquire a knowledge of the Four Noble Truths, they should at least attempt to obtain insight into the six *dhātus* (or basic constituent elements) of *paṭhavī*, *āpo*, *tejo*, *vāyo*, *ākāsa* and *viññāṇa*,[99] or insight into their fleeting and unstable nature—how they do not last for more than the twinkling of an eye at a time (so to say) and how they are continually being destroyed. They should attain to such insight through such methods of practice as studying, memorizing, reciting, reflecting, listening, discussing, questioning, practising insight exercises, and contemplating. If a clear insight is obtained into these six elements, there is no necessity for special practice with regard to the remaining *dhammas*.[100] If the nature of *anicca*, (impermanence) can be clearly realized, the realization of *anattā* (impersonality) follows as a matter of course.[101]

The realization of the nature of *dukkha* (suffering) can be accomplished in its entirety only when one attains the stage of *arahatta-phala* (fruition of holiness).

Thus, after putting forth effort for lengthy periods, when insight is obtained into the nature of the six elements both within and without oneself, as well as into the nature of their impermanence, fixed attention on them is achieved. This must be recognized as arising out of the predominant control exercised by *paññā*. The unreliability that had been a feature of one's mind throughout past infinite *saṃsāra* gradually disappears.

Here, "unreliability of one's mind" means the perception of permanency in things that are impermanent, of happiness in suffering,

---

99 The six elements: extension, liquidity or cohesion, fire or kinetic energy, wind or motion or support; space, and consciousness. On the meditation on the first four, see Ledi Sayādaw, *Magga Dipānī*, in the section "How to establish the Wisdom Group".

100 Such categories as aggregates (*khandha*) or sense-bases (*āyatana*).

101 See Udāna, Meghiya Vagga, Sutta 1: "In him who perceives impermanence the perception of not-self manifests itself. And he who perceives not-self obtains the elimination of the conceit "I am" and reaches Nibbāna in this very life".

of pleasantness in loathsomeness, of self in non-self, of individuals in non-individuals, of beings in non-beings, of humans in non-humans, of *devas*, Sakka and *brahmās* in non-*devas*, non-Sakka, and non-*brahmās*, of women, men, bullocks, buffaloes, elephants, horses in non-women, non-men, non-bullocks, non-buffaloes, non-elephants, and non-horses. Freedom from unreliability means perceiving the true reality after having obtained mastery over the mind within the Buddha Sāsana.

If *dukkha-sacca*, or the Noble Truth of Suffering, be clearly perceived, it follows as a matter of course that the other three truths can also be clearly perceived. In the perception of these four truths, the way that worldlings perceive them is known as "theoretical knowledge" (*anubodha*), while the way of the Noble (*ariya*, i.e., stream-enterers, etc.), is known as "penetrative understanding" (*paṭivedha*). "Theoretical knowledge" is like seeing a light at night but not the fire from which it originates. Although the fire cannot be directly seen, by seeing the reflected light one can know without doubt that there is a fire. Seeing the fire directly is like *paṭivedha*, the "penetrative understanding."

> *Saddhindriyaṃ bhāveti, viriyindriyaṃ bhāveti, satindriyaṃ bhāveti, samādhindriyaṃ bhāveti, paññindriyaṃ bhāveti.*[102]

The meaning of this Pāli passage uttered by the Buddha, is that the five *indriyas* (mental faculties) should be practiced and developed in order to facilitate the great work of *samatha* and *vipassanā*.

A person who has not developed these five *indriyas* is like a country without a ruler or king. It is like the forests and mountains inhabited by wild tribes where no administration exists. In a rulerless country there is no law. There the people are unrestrained. Like animals, the strong prey on the weak. In the same way, the mind of a person who has not developed the five *indriyas* is distracted and runs riot with defilements. Just as a person possessed by evil spirits cannot bear to hear the sound of such recitations as "*iti pi so*" or "*hetu paccayo*," when persons without developed *indriyas* hear talk connected with the cause of contentment (*paccaya-santosa*) or with the practice of mental development (*bhāvanārambha*), they quickly

102 Saṃyutta Nikāya, Mahā Vagga, Indriya Saṃyutta, Vagga 6, sutta 8.

discover antagonistic criticisms. In them, the desire to exert themselves in the work of *samatha* and *vipassanā* never arises.

On the other hand, a person who develops the five *indriyas* resembles a country ruled by a just and lawful king. It resembles the towns and hamlets of the *majjhima-desa* (central region) where governmental administration exists. Such a person is not disturbed by the variegated theories of various persons. He is confirmed in the sole way of the Buddha's teachings. When such a person hears talk connected with the cause of contentment, or the practice of mental development, his mind is clear and cool. He is confirmed in the desire to exert himself in the work of *samatha* and *vipassanā*.

In this way, the arising of the two kinds of desires in this world is not the work of beings or individuals, but depends on the existence or otherwise of development of the five *indriyas*. If there is no development of the *indriyas*, one kind of desire arises. If there is development of the *indriyas*, that desire disappears and a new kind of desire invariably appears. The more the development of the *indriyas* proceeds, the more does this new desire increase and gather strength. When all the five *indriyas* are set up, the desire for the paths and the fruits will immediately appear. Thus must beings develop the five *indriyas* in order to raise them from their ordinary level (*pakati-saddhā*, etc.) to the great heights of their developed (or meditative) plane (*bhāvanā-saddhā*, etc).

CHAPTER VI

THE FIVE MENTAL POWERS *(Bala)*

The mental powers (*balāni*) are thus called because "they overpower opposing mental states".[103] Or, as the commentaries explain: they are powerful in the sense of being unshaken (*akampanaṭṭhena*) by opposition.[104]

Parallel to the five faculties, there are five powers (*bala*):

1. *Saddhā*: faith
2. *Viriya*: energy
3. *Sati*: mindfulness
4. *Samādhi*: concentration
5. *Paññā*: wisdom

They are like five generals or commanders engaged in destroying the hostile kingdom of personality belief. They are the fivefold strength on which bhikkhus and layfolk can place their reliance.

As in the case of the faculties, the power of faith (*saddhā-bala*) is of two kinds: 1) The power of ordinary faith (*pakati-saddhā*), and 2) the power of developed faith (*bhāvanā-saddhā*).

"Ordinary faith," which has no development through specific practice, associates with *taṇhā* according to circumstances, and can thus produce only the ordinary good actions (*pakati-kusala-kamma*) of generosity or liberality, *dāna*, morality (*sīla*), etc. The limited measure of strength it possesses, cannot overcome craving. On the contrary, *taṇhā* keeps "ordinary faith" under its power.

The Pāli texts mention, with the great clarity, four[105] by "traditional practices of the Noble Ones" (*ariya-vaṃsa*). They are:

---

103 Paramattha Dīpanī, by Ledi Sayādaw.

104 Comy. to Aṅguttara-Nikāya, Ekaka-nipāta.

105 Aṅguttara-Nikāya, Catukka Nipāta (The Fours), Ariyavaṃsa-Sutta, translated in *With Robes and Bowl*, by Bhikkhu Khantipālo (*The Wheel* No. 83/84, p. 70).

1. Being easily satisfied with food
2. Being easily satisfied with clothing
3. Being easily satisfied with any dwelling place
4. Finding pleasure and enjoyment in the work of *bhāvanā* (meditation)

They constitute the realm of *saddhā*.[106] In the present day world, this great kingdom of *saddhā* lies hidden and submerged. Today, beings take pleasure and enjoyment in material things (*paccayāmisa*): they take pleasure and enjoyment in worldly rank, dignity, and honour (*lokāmisa*); they take pleasure and enjoyment in the attainment of the pleasant life, in worldly riches, and in power and dominion (*vaṭṭāmisa*); and thus is the great kingdom of *taṇhā* established as clearly as the great ocean round the island. This shows the weakness of ordinary faith (*pakati-saddhā*) in this world.

It is developed faith which, having its genesis in the successful practice of body contemplation (such as mindfulness of breathing) and being pursued until the disappearance of the distraction and unsettled condition of the mind, can dispel the craving which takes pleasure and enjoyment in the aforementioned three kinds of worldliness (*āmisa*). It is this developed faith (*bhāvanā-saddhā*) that can save bhikkhus and layfolk who are in the course of being drowned and submerged in the ocean of the three cravings,[107] and that enables them to reach the island haven of the kingdom of *saddhā*, as manifested (e.g.,) in the four traditional practices of the Noble Ones (*ariya-vaṃsa-dhamma*). In the context of the *bodhipakkhiya-dhamma* it is this developed faith that should be acquired.

Of the two kinds of energy (*viriya*), ordinary energy which is without development practice, is associated with laziness (*kosajja*) according to the occasion, and produces the ordinary good acts (*pakati-kusala-kamma*) of liberality or generosity, morality, the study of the sacred texts, etc. This ordinary energy cannot dispel laziness; on

---

106 This in the sense of confidence in these traditional values of simple living and mental culture, which in such a general formulation, apply also to lay followers. (Editor).

107 The three cravings are: sensual craving, craving for existence and craving for self-annihilation.

the contrary, it is laziness which controls ordinary energy and keeps it under subjection.

When beings encounter a Buddha Sāsana, they acquire the knowledge that in the past unfathomable *saṃsāra* they have been the kinsfolk of *sakkāya-diṭṭhi*, of evil deeds (*duccarita*) and the inhabitants of the lower worlds of misery (*apāya-loka*). The Pāli texts clearly prescribe the method of the *ariyavaṃsa*, the traditional practice of the Noble Ones, as a way of dispelling laziness; and the fourth of them, delight in meditation, should be practiced until release from such a state of laziness (being faith's opposite) is attained.

The way of dispelling laziness may be thus described (in the case of a monk).[108] Having equipped himself with the *sikkhās* (the training rules—which are the Buddha's heritage), which he has committed himself to in the ordination hall at the time of his becoming a bhikkhu, he:[109] makes the trees and bushes of the forest his dwelling-place, lives only on alms-food gathered on his alms-round, avoids company, observes the *dhutaṅga* and applies himself scrupulously to mindful body contemplation.

These are the acts of energy that dispel the unwholesome volitional actions (*akusala-kamma*) arising out of laziness (*kosajja*). They are acts comprised in the realm of energy.

This realm of energy remains obscure and is unknown in the present-day world. Today, although bhikkhus are aware that they belong to that class of beings still possessed of personality belief and evil deeds and liable to rebirth in lower worlds of misery, yet they live permanently in dwellings constructed in towns and villages by their donors; they take pleasure in the receipt of large gifts and benefits; they are unable to dispense with the company of other people, etc., all of which acts are comprised within the realm of laziness (*kosajja*) and this realm of laziness is as conspicuous as the sea that

108 In the case of layfolk, the principle underlying the four "Traditional practices" (*ariya-vaṃsa*) should be applied to their circumstances of life as strictly as possible. These principles may be summarized in a popular phrase as "simple living and high (meditative) thinking." (Editor).

109 For instance, the "four supports" (*nissaya*) of a monk's life, among which is the undertaking to live "at the foot of a tree" (though, in the same formula, monasteries, hermitages, etc., are also said to be permissible, that is for those unable to live the stricter life). (Editor).

inundates an island. This shows the weakness of ordinary energy (*pakati-viriya*).

It is only developed energy (*bhāvanā-viriya*)—such as being satisfied with a minimum of sleep, being always alert and active, being fearless, being bold and firm in living alone, being steadfast in meditative practice— that can dispel laziness. In the context of the *bodhipakkhiya-dhammā* it is this developed energy that should be acquired.

The detailed meaning of the powers of mindfulness, concentration and wisdom may be known by following the lines of explanation given above. Next I shall just give a more concise explanation.

The antithesis of mindfulness (*sati*) is *muṭṭhasacca*, confused mindfulness or absent-mindedness. It means inability to become absorbed in the work of tranquillity meditation (*samatha-bhāvanā*) or of insight meditation (*vipassanā-bhāvanā*); inability to concentrate and to control one's mind; the wandering of thoughts to objects other than the object of concentration. Ordinary mindfulness that one possesses in a rudimentary state from birth cannot dispel that absentmindedness. Only developed mindfulness can do it.

The antithesis of concentration (*samādhi*) is distraction (*vikkhepa*) of mind (i.e., wandering thoughts and idle fancies). It is the inability to concentrate, to control the mind and keep its attention fixed on one object. It is the arising of thoughts on objects other than the object of concentration. It is the unquiet and restless state of mind when applying itself to the work of meditation. Ordinary concentration cannot dispel the unwholesome state of distraction. Only developed concentration (*bhāvanā-samādhi*) can do it.

The antithesis of wisdom (*paññā*) is delusion (*sammoha*). It is ignorance, lack of clarity, vagueness and absence of lucidity of mind. It is the darkness shrouding the mind. This delusion cannot be removed by ordinary wisdom (*pakati-paññā*), nor by erudition (*pariyatti-paññā*), even if that comprises knowledge of the whole Tipiṭaka. It is only wisdom developed by meditation, (*bhāvanā-paññā*) that has set up mindful body contemplation, which can gradually dispel delusion.

This shows the meaning of the five unwholesome opposites (*paṭipakkha-akusala-dhamma*) coupled with the respective powers (*bala*).

These five unwholesome opposing forces are: 1) *taṇhā*; 2) laziness (*kosajja*), or inability to take pains (lassitude), or lack of fearlessness in Dhamma practice (*paṭipatti*), 3) absent-mindedness (*muṭṭha-sacca*), 4) distraction (*vikkhepa*), and 5) delusion (*sammoha*). The five things that can counteract and dispel them are called powers (*bala*). If any one of these powers is weak and unable to dispel the respective opposite, than meditation, be it tranquillity or insight, cannot be very successful as far as *neyya* individuals are concerned, i.e., those in need of guidance.

Hence, at the present day, some persons can emerge out of the realm of *taṇhā* because of the strength of their power of faith (*saddhā-bala*). They are rid of attachment to material things and to worldly dignities and honours. But as they are deficient in the other four powers, they are unable to rise above the stage of contentment (*santuṭṭhi*) with their living conditions.

Some persons can emerge out of the realm of craving and laziness because they are strong in the powers of faith and energy. They are constant in keeping to a life of contentment, and (if monks) firm in keeping to forest and hill dwellings and in the observance of the *dhutaṅga* as exemplifying their energy. But as they are weak in the other three powers, they are unable to practice mindful body contemplation, or do the work of tranquillity and insight meditation.

Some persons, again, are strong in the first three powers and thus can rise up to the work of mindful body contemplation (*kāyagatāsati*), achieving concentration, e.g., on out-and in-breath or in contemplating the bones of the body. But being deficient in the other two powers, they cannot rise up to the task of *jhāna* and insight.

Other persons can achieve the attainment of *jhāna* because they are strong in the first four powers, but as the power of wisdom is weak in them, they cannot rise to the work of insight.

Some persons are strong in the power of wisdom as far as their learning in Dhamma and Tipiṭaka is concerned. They are also wise in understanding the teachings on the ultimate realities (*paramattha dhamma*). But because they lack the backing of the other four powers they cannot emerge from the realm of craving, lassitude, absentmindedness and distraction. They live and die within the confines of these unwholesome states. In this way, whenever one is deficient in any one of the powers, one cannot rise above the realm of the respective opposite force.

Of the five powers, those of energy and wisdom are also *iddhipādas*, "bases of (spiritual) success." Hence, if these two powers are strong and coordinated, it does not happen that one cannot rise up to the work of insight (*vipassanā*) because of the weakness of the other three powers.

People who do not know the functions of the bases of success, the controlling faculties (*indriya*) and the powers (*bala*), do not know why their zeal is weak and which are the opposing forces (*paṭipakkha*) that assail them. They do not know the qualities of mind which they have to cultivate, and hence the desire to cultivate them never arises. It is thus that the traditional practices of the Noble Ones (*ariya-vaṃsa*) are on the verge of disappearing at the present day.

I shall give an illustration. There is a species of bull called usabha. It is a bull worth more than a thousand ordinary bulls. If the characteristics and distinctive signs of that bull be recognized, and it be reared and nurtured properly, its limbs and marks will develop, and its strength and powers will increase. It can then guard even a hundred cattle pens from the incursions of lions and leopards.

If the owner of such a bull is ignorant of its potential, and if thus he does not rear and nurture it properly but keeps and tends it just as he would any other ordinary bull; if he employs it in ploughing and drawing carts in company with other bulls; then its distinctive marks and limbs will fail to develop and its strength and powers will remain dormant. It will thus live and die just like any other bull.

A knowing owner, however, will separate such a bull from the rest and keep it in a specially constructed shed. He will cover the floor of the shed with clean sand and will fix a ceiling to the roof. He will keep the shed clean and will feed the bull with paddy and pulses fit for human consumption. He will wash and bathe it. In such a case, the distinctive marks and limbs will develop, and its strength and powers will increase enormously.

In this Buddha Sāsana, *neyya* individuals (requiring guidance) resemble the owner of the bull. The five powers of these *neyya* individuals resemble the usabha bull. The Satipaṭṭhāna Vibhaṅga, Sammāpadhāna Vibhaṅga, Iddhipāda Vibhaṅga, Indriya Vibhaṅga, Bojjjhaṅga Vibhaṅga, and Maggaṅga Vibhaṅga, of the Abhidhamma Piṭaka, and the Mahāsatipaṭṭhāna Sutta, Satipaṭṭhāna Saṃyutta, Indriya Saṃyutta, Bala Saṃyutta, and Bojjhaṅga Saṃyutta of the Sutta Piṭaka, resemble the expository books which expound the distinctive signs, marks and characteristics of usabha bulls, the methods how such bulls are to be reared and taken care of, and the strength and powers that such bulls can attain if reared and nurtured properly.

Those *neyya* individuals who through ignorance do not attempt to develop the five powers through the work of meditation and who thus remain satisfied with the lower attainments within the Sāsana, such as *dāna*, *sīla*, and the study of scriptures (*pariyatti*), resemble the ignorant owner of an usabha bull who does not rear and nurture it properly.

In this world, there are many kinds of worldly undertakings. There are undertakings that can be accomplished by the strength of wealth, and there are undertakings that can be accomplished by the strength of knowledge. Even in the case of the cultivation of land, several kinds of strength are needed for its accomplishment. Sometimes the strength of wealth has to be gathered first, and at other times the strength of knowledge. Preparatory education and study constitute the gathering of the strength of knowledge.

Similarly, in the Buddha Sāsana, there are five powers needed for the work of *samatha*, *vipassanā*, and the attainment of the holy paths and fruits and Nibbāna. It is only when these powers are first brought together that the great works mentioned can be undertaken. Those persons who do not possess even one of the five powers cannot evoke a desire to undertake these great tasks. It does not occur to them that those great tasks can be accomplished in this life. They live forgetfully and without determination. If it is pointed out to them that the tasks can be accomplished, they do not wish to hear it. They do not know that such untoward thoughts occur to them because they are utterly impoverished in their spiritual powers. They lay the blame at the door of *pāramī*, or *dvi-hetuka*, or at the unfavorable times.[110]

If, however, these people set up work in one of the *satipaṭṭhāna*, such as in *ānāpānasati*, and if thereby they set up the three powers of *saddhā*, *viriya*, and *sati*, such untoward thoughts will certainly disappear. It is inevitable that new wholesome thoughts must arise. This is because they have developed their strength.

This is how the strength is developed. Although such a person cannot as yet attain an insight into body and mind, the weak faith grows through the control exercised over craving for material wants (*paccayāmisa*) and worldly achievements (*lokāmisa*). The weak energy grows through control of lassitude. Weak mindfulness grows through control of absent-mindedness. Concentration and wisdom, too, gather strength through control of distraction and delusion. When these powers grow, it is inevitable that there must be a change in the mind of the meditator.

A person who is afflicted with a major disease has no desire to take an interest in the ordinary affairs and activities of the world. But if, after taking proper medicine and treatment, his grave illness is gradually cured and he is aroused from his apathy, it is inevitable that he will again take interest in normal activities. Here, the five unwholesome opposing forces, i.e., craving, lassitude, etc., resemble major diseases. The work of tranquillity and insight meditation resembles the affairs and activities of the world. Work in the field of *satipaṭṭhāna*, such as mindfulness of breathing, resembles the proper medicines and treatment taken. The rest of this comparison can be easily understood.

Hence did the Buddha say: "He develops the powers of faith, energy, mindfulness, concentration and wisdom." ("*saddhābalaṃ bhāveti*...")

In this world, the strength of builders lies in good tools, such as awls, chisels, axes, knives, saws, etc. Only when equipped with such

---

110 Some believe that these are times when the holy paths and the fruits thereof can no longer be attained, and tend to defer effort till the *pāramis* ripen. Some believe that persons of the present day are *dvi-hetuka* (i.e., beings reborn with two root-conditions only, namely detachment and amity), and as such they cannot attain the holy paths and the fruits thereof in the present life.

tools can they undertake to build. Similarly, in the Sāsana, the tools of tranquillity and insight meditation (*samatha*) and (*vipassanā*) for achieving the knowledge of the paths and fruitions of Sainthood (*magga-* and *phala-ñāṇā*) consist of developed faith, developed energy, developed mindfulness, developed concentration and developed wisdom (*bhāvanā-saddhā*, etc.), which are developed through one of the *satipaṭṭhānas*, such as mindfulness of breathing. These five powers are the strength of meditators (*yogāvacara*). Hence these five powers must be developed in order to undertake successfully the work of tranquillity and insight meditation within the Buddha Sāsana. This is the meaning of the word *bhāveti* (he develops) in the text quoted above.

CHAPTER VII

The Seven Factors Of Enlightenment *(Bojjhaṅga)*

Catusaccadhamme suṭṭhu bujjhati'ti sambodhi; sambodhiyā aṅgo sambojjhaṅgo.

The word-explanation given above, means: because *sambodhi* fully awakens to the Four Truths, therefore it is called "awakenment" (or enlightenment). *Sambodhi* signifies here the knowledge of the supramundane path (*lokuttara-magga-ñāṇa*). A constituent of such path knowledge is called a factor of enlightenment.

Birds are first delivered from their mothers' wombs in the form of eggs. By breaking through the shells, they are then delivered for a second time. Finally, when they become fully fledged with feathers and wings, they are delivered from their nests and can fly wherever they please. Similarly in the case of meditators, they are first delivered from the distractions of mind which have accompanied them throughout beginningless *saṃsāra*, successfully setting up mindful body contemplation or by accomplishing the work of tranquillity meditation. Secondly, when they attain insight (*vipassanā*) into body, mind, aggregates (*rūpa, nāma, khandhā*) etc., they are free from coarse forms of ignorance. Finally, when the seven factors of enlightenment (*bojjhaṅga*), develop and mature, they become fully fledged by attaining the knowledge of the supramundane path (*lokuttara-magga-ñāṇa*) called *sambodhi*, and thus they are delivered from the state of worldlings (*puthujjana*), attaining the state of *ariya*, i.e., of the supramundane (*lokuttara*) or Nibbāna.

There are seven *bojjhaṅgas*, or the factors of enlightenment:

1. *Sati-sambojjhāṅga*: mindfulness
2. *Dhammavicaya-sambojjhaṅga*: investigation of Dhamma
3. *Viriya-sambojjhaṅga*: energy
4. *Pīti-sambojjhaṅga*: joy
5. *Passaddhi-sambojjhaṅga*: tranquillity

6. *Samādhi-sambojjhaṅga*: concentration
7. *Upekkhā sambojjhaṅga*: equanimity

The mental factor "mindfulness" (*sati-cetasika*), called diversely *satipaṭṭhāna*, *satindriya*, *sati-bala*, *sammā-sati*, *maggaṅga*, this is *sati-sambojjhaṅga*, the enlightenment factor "mindfulness."

The mental factor "wisdom" (*paññā-cetasika*), diversely called *vīmaṃsiddhipāda*, *paññindriya*, *paññā-bala*, *sammādiṭṭhi-maggaṅga*, all are *dhammavicaya-sambojjhaṅga*, the enlightenment factor "investigation of Dhamma." Alternatively, the five purifications pertaining to wisdom, the knowledge of the three contemplations, the ten insight knowledges,[111] are also called *dhammavicaya-sambojjhaṅga*. Just as cotton seeds are milled, carded, etc., so as to produce cotton wool, the process of repeatedly viewing the five aggregates (*khandha*) in the light of *vipassanā-ñāṇa* (insight knowledge) is called *dhammavicaya-sambojjhaṅga*, the enlightenment factor "investigation of Dhamma."

The mental factor "energy" (*viriya-cetasika*), called diversely *sammāpadhāna*, *viriyiddhipāda*, *viriyindriya*, *viriyiyabala*, and *sammā-vāyāma maggaṅga*, these are *viriya-sambojjhaṅga*, the enlightenment factor "energy."

The joy and happiness that appears when the process of (truly) seeing and knowing increases by the practice of *satipaṭṭhāna*, e.g., by mindful body contemplation, is called *pīti-sambojjhaṅga*, the enlightenment factor "joy."

The process of becoming calm and tranquil in both body and mind when the mental distractions, reflections and thoughts abate, is called *passaddhi-sambojjhaṅga*, the enlightenment factor "tranquillity." It is the mental factor (*cetasika*) of tranquillity of body and of mind (*kāya-passaddhi*, *citta-passadhi*).

The factors pertaining to concentration, called *samādhindriya*, *samādhi-bala*, and *sammā-samādhi-maggaṅga*, are *samādhi-sambojjhaṅga*, the enlightenment factor "concentration." Alternatively, preliminary access and full concentration, or the eight *jhānas*, associated with the work of tranquillity (*samatha*) and purification of mind (*citta-visuddhi*) and voidness concentration (*suññatā-samādhi*) etc., associated with the purifications pertaining to wisdom, are

111 See notes 91, 92 and 93.

also called *samādhi-sambojjhaṅga.* The concentration that accompanies insight knowledge (*vipassanā-ñāṇa*), or the knowledge of the paths and fruitions is called voidness concentration (*suññatā-samādhi*), conditionless concentration (*animitta-samādhi*) and desireless concentration (*appaṇihita-samādhi*).

When work on the subject of meditation (*kammaṭṭhāna*) is not yet methodical or systematic, much effort has to be exercised both bodily and mentally. But when the work becomes methodical and systematic, one is freed from such effort. This freedom is called *tatramajjhattatā-cetasika*, the mental factor of equipoise. And this is *upekkhā-sambojjhaṅga*, the enlightenment factor of equanimity.

When a meditator becomes endowed with these seven characteristics of *sambodhi* equally, he enjoys the happiness and joy of a monk (*samaṇa*) in the Buddha Sāsana—a happiness and joy unequalled and unparalleled by any worldly pleasure. Thus it is said in the Dhammapada:

> The bhikkhu who has retired to a lonely abode
> and has calmed his mind,
> experiences joy transcending that of men,
> as he clearly perceives the Dhamma.
>
> Whenever he reflects on the rise and fall of the aggregates,
> he experiences joy and happiness.
> To "those who know"
> that (reflection) is the Deathless.

Verses 373, 374

There are texts and stories wherein it is related that ailments and major diseases have been cured by the mere listening to the recitation of these seven factors of enlightenment.[112] But these ailments and diseases can be cured only when the listeners are fully aware of the meaning of these factors, and great and clear *saddhā* (faith) arises in them.

When these seven factors of enlightenment are acquired in a balanced manner, the meditator can rest assured that there will be no deficiency in his mindfulness directed to the body (*kāyagatāsati*); no deficiency in his perception of impermanence and not-self nor in his

112 See Bojjhaṅga Saṃyutta Nikāya.

mental and bodily energy (*viriya*). Because his mind is set at rest in regard to these three factors (*sati*, *dhammavicaya*, *viriya*), he experiences joy (*pīti*) in the knowledge that he can now perceive the light of Nibbāna which had never appeared to him in the beginningless past *saṃsāra*, not even in his dreams. Because of that joy and ease (*sukha*) of mind, his application to the *kammaṭṭhāna* objects becomes calm and steady (*passaddhi*), and equanimity (*upekkhā*) arises, which is free from the anxieties and efforts for mindfulness (*sati*), perception of *anicca* and *anattā* (*dhammavicaya*) and the necessity to rouse energy (*viriya*).

All the above statements are made with reference to the stage at which the factors of enlightenment are in unison with one another and their respective functions are well performed. But even at the stage of ordinary practice, from the moment mindfulness directed to the body is set up, qualities such as mindfulness are known as *bojjhangas* (factors of enlightenment).

The Enlightened One has said (in the Bojjhaṅga Saṃyutta):

> *Satisambojjhaṅgaṃ bhāveti, vivekanissitaṃ, virāganissitaṃ nirodhanissitaṃ, vossaggapariṇāmiṃ; dhammavicaya-sambojjhaṅgaṃ...upekkhā-sambojjhaṅgaṃ bhāveti, vivekanissitaṃ virāganissitaṃ nirodhanissitaṃ vossagga-pariṇāmiṃ.*
>
> "He develops the enlightenment factors "mindfulness ... equanimity, dependent on detachment, on absence of lust, on cessation, and culminating in relinquishment."

This means that, in the ordinary course (referred to by the words "He develops ...") the process of setting up mindful body contemplation amounts to the setting up of the seven factors of enlightenment. The distinctive and higher cultivation of them is indicated by the words "dependent on detachment ..."[113]

The meaning of the Pāli passage quoted above, is: One should practice the enlightenment factors mindfulness (etc.). This is dependent on the absence of all other activities and anxieties, on the absence of lust and greed, of the suffering attendant upon the round of rebirths and on the relinquishment of the four substrata of existence (*upadhi*).[114]

---

113 Explained in the Commentary to the Bojjhaṅga Vibhaṅga.

114 The four substrata of existence are 1) sense pleasures (*kāmūpadhi*),

CHAPTER VIII

THE EIGHT PATH FACTORS *(Maggaṅga)*

The eight factors or constituents of the path are:

1. Right view (*sammā-diṭṭhi*) 2. Right thought (*sammā-saṅkappa*)	Wisdom (*paññā*)
3. Right speech (*sammā-vācā*) 4. Right action (*sammā-kammanta*) 5. Right livelihood (*sammā-ājīva*)	Morality *(sīla)*
6. Right effort (*sammā-vāyāma*) 7. Right mindfulness (*sammā-sati*) 8. Right concentration(*sammā-samādhi*)	Concentration *(samādhi)*

All these eight path factors are present in the supramundane purification by knowledge and vision (*lokuttara-ñāṇadassana-visuddhi*). In the preceding mundane purifications, right speech, right action and right livelihood are present only in the purification of virtue (*sīla-visuddhi*). They are not present in purification of mind (*citta-visuddhi*) and the rest.

Morality *(Sīla)*

Hence, in the context of the requisites of enlightenment , purification of virtue (*sīla-visuddhi*) is by nature "dependent on detachment" (*viveka-nissita*), etc., in accordance with the following text (from the Maggaṅga Vibhaṅga):

---

2) mental defilements (*kilesūpadhi*), 3) *kamma* (*kammūpadhi*), and 4) the five aggregates (*khandhūpadhi*).

"He develops right speech, dependent on detachment, dependent on absence of lust, dependent on cessation, culminating in relinquishment. He develops right action ... right livelihood, dependent on detachment ..."

It does not refer to virtue (*sīla*) that has leanings towards happy forms of existence (*bhava-sampatti*) and depends on the round of rebirths (*vaṭṭa-nissita*). The *sīla-visuddhi* of those who have consciously given up attempts at attaining the holy paths and fruits in this life, is not genuine *ādibrahmacariyaka-sīla*, "virtue belonging to the essence of the holy life," and thus is not of the genuine *bodhipakkhiya* class. If effort be made, however, towards the attainment of Nibbāna in the next life, it can be *pāramī-sīla*, which is part of *vivaṭṭanissita-sīla*, "virtue tending towards the ending of the round of rebirths."

The path factors of right speech, right action and right livelihood are purely of the class of morality (*sīlakkhandha*) and hence constitute genuine perfection of virtue. They are also called the three *virati-cetasikā*, mental factors of (vocal and bodily) abstention.

Right thought (*sammā-saṅkappa*) is the mental factor "thought-conception" (*vitakka-cetasika*). As it is the harbinger of wisdom, it is included in the wisdom category (*paññā-kkhandha*) of the eightfold path. It is threefold, namely: thoughts of renunciation, of non-hate and non-harming (*nekkhamma-*, *abyāpāda-*, and *avihiṃsā-saṅkappa*). Just as a person incarcerated in prison or besieged by enemy troops or encircled by forest fire, or as a fish caught in a net, tank or trap, or a bird caught in a cage, will be absorbed (without being able to sleep or eat) in the one thought how to escape from these confinements, so are the attempts of persons who contrive with energy of the *sammāpadhāna*-types to escape from the confinement of the old and infinitely numerous "unwholesome *kamma* arisen in the past" (*upanna-akusala-kamma*) and the new infinitely numerous "unwholesome *kamma* not yet arisen, (*anuppanna-akusala-kamma*) that is due to arise in the future. The thoughts of such a person are the path factor "thoughts of renunciation" (*nekkhamma-saṅkappa-maggaṅga*). It is the sort of thought which looks for the way to escape from the sufferings of the round of rebirths (*vaṭṭa-dukkha*).

The thought that associates with *mettā jhāna* is called *abyāpāda-saṅkappa*, "the thought of non-hate"; if associated with *karuṇā-jhāna*, it is called *avihiṃsā-saṅkappa*, "the thought of non-harming." The thought that associates with the remaining *jhānas* is called "thought of renunciation."

The four path factors of right view, right effort, right mindfulness and right concentration have been dealt with in the chapter on the enlightenment factors.

The *ājīvaṭṭhamaka-sīla* (see note 20) that is taken and observed with the purpose of destroying the great kingdom of *diṭṭhi-anusaya* (proclivity to wrong views) belongs to the path factors of the mundane morality category (*lokiya-sīlakkhandha-maggaṅga*). It is also purification of virtue.

That eightfold virtue ending with right livelihood (*ājīvaṭṭhamaka-sīla*) is twofold: for layfolk and for monks. Abstention from the threefold evil conduct in deeds (*kāyaduccarita*) and fourfold in words (*vacī-duccarita*) comprise that virtue for layfolk. The eight or ten precepts (see notes 21 and 22) are refinements of that virtue.

For monks, that virtue is constituted by the observance of the 227 Vinaya rules, which cover bodily and vocal *kamma*. The remaining rules laid down in the Vinaya Piṭaka are refinements of it.

Just as trees grow in the soil, so the last six purifications beginning with purification of mind, develop in the soil of the first, the purification of virtue (*sīla-visuddhi*). In particular, the purification of virtue does not mix with the five middle (mundane) purifications, but supports them by securing antecedent purity. In the case of the seventh purification, the supramundane purification of knowledge and vision, the purification of virtue operates in conjunction with it, being identical with the three constituents of the morality group (*sīlakkhandha*) of the (supramundane) eightfold path. The reason is that, in the case of the purification of virtue, the objects of attention are different from those of the five middle purifications; but they are identical with those of the supramundane purification, operating together with it as coexistent (*saha-jāta*).

Concentration *(Samādhi)*

With reference to the *samādhi* category of the path, there are two courses of action. Firstly, the way of one who practices pure insight only (*suddha-vipassanā-yānika*). He, after fulfilling purity of virtue and setting up mindful body contemplation, does not follow the way of tranquillity but the way of pure insight such as purification of view, etc. Secondly, there is the course of one who practices both tranquillity and insight (*samatha-vipassanā-yānika*). He, after attaining the first *jhāna* etc., takes up the practice of insight, by way of purification of view, etc.

Of these two: 1) In the practice of pure insight, the three path factors of the concentration category (*samādhikkhandha*) fulfill the functions of tranquillity and purification of mind (*citta-visuddhi*), through the three kinds of concentration known as emptiness concentration, conditionless and desireless concentration. 2) In the practice of tranquillity followed by insight, the three path factors of the concentration category fulfill the functions of tranquillity and purification of mind, by way of the three stages of concentration, namely preparatory concentration (*parikamma-samādhi*), access concentration (*upacāra-samādhi*) and full concentration (*paṇā-samādhi*); and thereafter, at the insight stage, the above two functions are fulfilled by emptiness concentration, etc.

During the period of the preceding practice of purity of virtue and of mindful body contemplation, however, the three constituents of the concentration category fulfil the functions of momentary concentration (*khaṇika-samādhi*).

Wisdom *(Paññā)*

The two constituents of the wisdom category fulfil the functions of wisdom in the ways of both the practice of pure insight and that preceded by tranquillity, after the setting up of the purification of virtue and of mindful body contemplation. These remarks apply to both the mundane and the supramundane path factors.

Stream-entry (*Sotāpatti*)

I shall now show the path of stream-entry (*sotāpatti-magga*) in the supramundane path factors. It should be remembered that this book is aimed at the lowest of the stages of sanctity, namely the "Bon-sin-san" *sukkhavipassaka-sotāpanna* (see note 64). At the present time there are countless numbers of beings such as Visākhā, Anāthapiṇḍika, Sakka the ruler of Devas, the four Divine Great Kings (*cātummahārājika-deva*) etc., who still continue to derive pleasure and ease within the round of rebirths, inhabiting their respective celestial abodes. They are beings who have before them seven more rebirths in the sense-desire worlds (including the lower celestial worlds of the sense sphere) and one rebirth each in the six worlds on the level of the fourth *jhāna* or the Vehapphala *brahma* worlds. The number of births in the *brahma* worlds of the first, second and third *jhāna* is undetermined.

Why are they called stream-enterers (*sotāpanna*)? The five great rivers and the five hundred lesser ones that have their source in the Himalayas, do not flow up, but flow continuously down to the great ocean. Hence they are called *sota* (stream or current). Similarly, *ariya* do not fall back to the state of worldlings but proceed continuously (as *ariyas*) until they attain Anupādisesa-Nibbāna (where "here is no remainder of the aggregates of existence). In the case of the worldlings, although they may attain rebirth in the highest celestial worlds, they possess still the liability to be reborn in the lowest *avīci* hell. But in the case of *ariyas*, wherever they may be reborn, they do not fall into the lower worlds of misery, but possess a continuous tendency of being reborn in a higher world. Though worldlings may attain the state of *tihetuka brahmas*[115] in the fine-material (*rūpa*) or non-material (*arūpa*) worlds, they still possess the liability of being reborn in an unhappy from of existence (*duggati*) as *ahetuka*[116] creatures such as dogs or pigs.

115 The term *tihetuka* refers to rebirth consciousness having all three wholesome root conditions (*hetu*), i.e., non-greed, non-hate, and non-delusion.

116 *Ahetuka* refers to a rebirth consciousness without any of the three wholesome root conditions.

Whether it be the place of rebirth or the status attained in each rebirth, noble ones (*ariya*) do not regress, but proceed higher and higher from one world to the next, or from one status to another, until after many rebirths and many worlds have passed, they reach the highest worlds and the highest status, when they discard the five aggregates entirely and attain to Anupādisesa-Nibbāna. The process by which this straight path of ascent is traversed is called *dhammasota*, the stream of Dhamma. It comprises the stream of right view (*sammā-diṭṭhi-sota*) the stream of right thought (*sammā-saṅkappa-sota*) and so forth up to the stream of right concentration (*sammā-samādhi-sota*).

The "stream of right view" means the establishment of the great realm of right view (*sammā-diṭṭhi*) where the light of the Four Noble Truths can be clearly perceived. This great realm of right view is established by replacing the great *anusaya* plane of *sakkāya-diṭṭhi*, the proclivity for personality-belief.

This resembles the rising of the sun after the night is over, when darkness is dispelled and light is established. In the same way the great kingdom of light of right view remains established throughout many lives and many world cycles until the attainment of Anupādisesa-Nibbāna. This light increases and becomes more and more firmly established from one rebirth to another.

It also resembles a person born blind due to cataracts covering both his eyes, who, on receiving good treatment, is cured of the cataract and gains sight. From the moment the cataract disappears, the view of the earth, the mountains, the sky with sun, moon and stars, etc, is opened to him and remains so throughout his life. Similarly, the noble stream-enterers (*sotāpanna-ariya*) gain the view of the three characteristics of existence (*ti-lakkhaṇa*) and of the Four Noble Truths, and do not lose it. This is how the path factor "right view" is firmly established.

The canonical text says:[117]

Sammā-diṭṭhassa sammā-saṅkappo pahoti.[118]

In him who has right view, right thought progresses.

117 Magga Saṃyutta, 1,1.

118 According to the Commentary, the word *pahoti* has the meaning of *vaddhati*, to grow, to increase.

According to this, if right view is established, also right thought, which consists of intention and plan to escape from worldly ills (*nekkhamma*) and to protect others from harm and suffering, becomes established and thrives from one rebirth to another until the attainment of the final goal. This is how right thought is established.

Sammā-saṅkappassa sammā-vācā pahoti.

In him who has right thought, right speech progresses.

When the intention and plan to escape from worldly ills and to see others happy and unharmed is established, there will be right speech free from the four faults (the *vacī-duccarita*) and this will become progressively established. This is how right speech is established.

Sammā-vācassa sammā-kammanto pahoti.

In him who has right speech, right action progresses.

If speech free from verbal misconduct is established, bodily acts free from the threefold bodily misconduct (*kāyaduccarita*) will become progressively established. This is how right action is established.

Sammā-kammantassa sammā-ājīvo pahoti.

In him who has right action, right livelihood progresses.

When views, intentions, speech and acts become pure, the forms of livelihood will also be pure and one will never resort to low and base forms of livelihood. This is how right livelihood is established.

Sammā-ājīvassa sammā-vāyāmo pahoti.

In him who has right livelihood, right effort progresses.

When views, intentions, speech, acts and livelihood become pure, energy and effort of a kind that is never devoted to misconduct or wrong livelihood becomes permanently established. This is how right effort is established.

Sammā-vāyāmassa sammā-sati pahoti.

In him who has right effort, right mindfulness progresses.

Similarly, right mindfulness that has its root in the efforts for morality, concentration and wisdom, becomes firmly established from one rebirth to another. This is how right mindfulness is established.

> *Sammā-satissa sammā-samādhi pahoti.*
>
> In him who has right mindfulness, right concentration progresses.

In the same way right concentration which is rooted in mindful attention to the work of morality, concentration and wisdom also becomes permanently established and thus becomes endowed with great power over the mind. This is how Right concentration is established.

It is in this way that the eight path factors (*maggaṅga*), called *dhamma* streams (*dhamma-sota*), become progressively established throughout many lives and many worlds, from the moment a being attains the stage of a stream-enterer (*sotāpanna*) until he finally attains Anupādisesa-Nibbāna.

Although from the moment when body contemplation is set up, there is such progress as has been shown earlier, yet so long as the state of stability (or constancy of progress; *niyāma*) is not reached, that being is not as yet a Noble One (*ariya*). It is the path of stream-entry (*sotāpatti-magga*) that is the starting point of the *ariya-sota*, the holy stream. As soon as beings reach the path of stream-entry, they enter the domain of the noble ones. Hence it is said:

> *Sotam ādito pajjiṃsu pāpuṇiṃsu'ti soṭāpannā.*
>
> They are called stream-enterers as they enter or reach the holy stream for the first time.

This ends our answer to the question, "Why are they called *sotāpannas*?"

As soon as beings reach the stage of Noble Ones, they transcend the state of worldlings. They are no longer beings of the "world", the mundane (*lokiya*), but have become beings of the supramundane (*lokuttara*). They are no longer committed to the sufferings of the round of rebirths (*vaṭṭa-dukkha*), having become "beings of Nibbāna". Throughout the series of many existences that may still be before them, they will never fall back from the first stage of their realization of Nibbāna, which they have achieved as stream-enterers. They are no longer liable to return to the *anusaya* plane of *sākkāya-diṭṭhi*, the proclivity for personality belief, or to the state of worldlings. They are firmly established on the first stage of *sa-upādisesa-nibbāna*, the Nibbāna realized during life-time, and will, during their remaining existences, enjoy at will the happiness of humans, *devas* and *brahmās*.

These eight path factors occur simultaneously to these noble ones only at the instant of their attainment of a path or a fruition (i.e., in supramundane consciousness). Where, however, mundane wholesome volitional acts (*lokiya-kusalakamma*) are concerned, the three constituents of the *sīla* category associate only with *sīla-kusala-kamma*. But the three constituents of the *samādhi* category and the two of the *paññā* category associate with many kinds of *kusala kamma*.

Although the three path factors of the *sīla* category associate only with *sīla-kusala-kamma*, they are firmly established in noble ones as "non-contravention" (*avītikkama*) throughout their remaining lives.[119]

---

119 The "pure phenomena" (*sobhana-cetasika*) involved in the thirty-seven *bodhipakkhiya-dhamma* are 14, namely: (1) zeal or desire, (2) consciousness (*citta*), (3) equipoise (*tatramajjhattatā* or *upekkhā*, (4) faith (*saddhā*), (5) tranquillity (*passaddhi*), (6) wisdom (*paññā*), (7) thought-conception (*vitakka* or *saṅkappa*), (8) effort (*viriya*), (9) right speech (*sammā-vācā*), (10) right action (*sammā-kammanta*), (11) right livelihood (*sammā-ājīva*), (12) mindfulness (*sati*), (13) joy (*pīti*), (14) one-pointedness of mind (*ekaggatā* or *samādhi*).

CHAPTER IX

How To Practice The *Bodhipakkhiya Dhammas*

Beings who encounter a Buddha Sāsana have to set up purification of virtue (*sīla-visuddhi*) first and then strive to acquire the requisites of enlightenment (*bodhipakkhiya-dhamma*), in order to enter the stream of the noble ones (*ariya-sota*).

I shall now give a brief description of how the practice should be undertaken.

The practice of the seven purifications (*satta visuddhi*) amounts to practising the *bodhipakkhiya-dhammas*.

In particular, the purification of mind concerns only persons who follow the way of tranquillity practice.[120]

The purification of knowledge and vision of what is and what is not path" (*maggāmagga-ñāṇadassana-visuddhi*) concerns only those highly conceited (or self-deceiving) persons (*adhimānika*)[121] who think that they have attained to the holy paths and the fruits when really they have no such attainment.

The purification of virtue, the purification by overcoming doubt, the purification by knowledge and vision of the way, the supramundane purification by knowledge and vision, all these apply to many different types of persons.

Of these five purifications, that of virtue has been dealt with in the chapter on the path factors, under the *sīla* category. It consists of keeping the "precepts that have right livelihood as the eighth" (*ājīvaṭṭhamaka-sīla*).

Purification of mind may be undertaken by practicing mindful body contemplation. For that purpose, some take up mindfulness of breathing and, generally, it may be said that if attention can rest on

120 According to the *Visuddhimagga*, also access concentration (*upacāra-samādhi*) is included in *citta-visuddhi*. It is this quality of concentration that is required of insight meditation. (Editor)

121 See the kindred term *abhimānika*, explained in *The Wheel* 61/62, p.43 (Note 3 to the Discourse on Effacement). (Editor)

the out-and-in-breath whenever one wishes and in whatever the bodily posture may by, then mindful body contemplation is established. Some persons practice that contemplation by way of the four postures of the body (*iriyāpatha*), in accordance with the text in the Satipaṭṭhāna Sutta: "When going, he is aware "I am going"", etc. Others take up clear comprehension (*sati-sampajañña*) of bodily activities. Others, practice body contemplation by attention to the thirty-two parts of the body. The first five are hair of the head, hair of the body, nails, teeth, skin, and are called *taca-pañcaka*, the skin pentad. If attention can be firmly and steadily placed on these parts at will, in a bodily posture, body contemplation is established. Attention can also be directed to the bones of the body. Body contemplation will be established if attention can be steadily and firmly placed on the bones of the head (skull). If, from the beginning, the physical and mental processes (*nāma-rūpa*) connected with the body (i.e., its functions and the attention given to all these processes) can be analytically discerned, and if attention to such work is firm and steady, the work of body contemplation is accomplished. This gives concisely the method of mindful body contemplation.

The work of purification of view (*diṭṭhi-visuddhi*) can be considered accomplished if the six elements (*dhātu*, see note 99) can be analytically perceived.

In the work of the purification by overcoming doubt (*kaṅkhāvitaraṇa-visuddhi*), if the causes for the appearance of the six elements mentioned above can be clearly perceived, it is accomplished. It must be clearly perceived that the causes for the appearance of *paṭhavi*, *āpo*, *tejo*, *vāyo* and *ākāsa* (the first five elements) are *kamma*, consciousness (*citta*), temperature (*utu*) and nutriment (*āhāra*),[122] and that the causes for the appearance of the six types of consciousness (*citta*—the sixth element) are the corresponding six objects of perception.

By the purification by knowledge and vision of the way (*paṭipadā-ñāṇadassana-visuddhi*) is meant the three characteristics of impermanence, suffering and not-self. If these are clearly perceived in the six elements mentioned above, this purification is attained.

---

122 See *Manual of Insight* (*Wheel* 31/32), p. 47.

The supramundane purification by knowledge and vision (*lokuttara-ñāṇadassana-visuddhi*) consists of the knowledge pertaining to the four holy paths of stream-entry, etc.; (*magga-ñāṇa*).

This shows concisely the five (middle) purifications.

CHAPTER X

The Heritage Of The Sāsana[123]

These thirty-seven requisites of enlightenment, treated in the preceding chapters, are the heritage of the Buddha. They are the heritage of the Sāsana. They constitute gems of the Sāsana that are priceless and invaluable.

I shall now examine what constitutes this heritage of the Sāsana (*sāsana-dāyajja*).

By "heritage" is meant property given as legacy by parents to their children who are fit to receive it as heirs (*dāyāda*). This applies also to the heritage of the Sāsana which is the Buddha's heritage (Buddha-*dāyajja*).

As to the nature of that heritage, there are two kinds: worldly (*āmisa*) and Dhamma heritage.

The worldly heritage consists of the four requisites of a bhikkhu, namely, alms-food, robes, dwelling place, and medicines. The Dhamma heritage are the three trainings (*sikkhā*, *sīla*, *samādhi*, *paññā*), the seven purifications, and the thirty-seven requisites of enlightenment.

There are two kinds of Dhamma heritage, namely mundane (*lokiya*) and supramundane (*lokuttara*). The mundane one consists of the above three trainings on the mundane level, the six mundane purifications and the requisites of enlightenment as far as associated with those mundane purifications. The supramundane Dhamma heritage consists of the three trainings on the supramundane level, the supramundane seventh purification, and the supramundane requisites of enlightenment.

Mundane Dhamma heritage may be divided into 1) that dependent on the round of rebirths (*vaṭṭa-nissita*), and 2) that tending towards the ending of the round of rebirths (*vivaṭṭa-nissita*); Or into 1) stable Dhamma heritage (*niyata*), and 2) unstable Dhamma heritage (*aniyata*)

123 This chapter has been abridged. (Editor)

The practice of the three trainings (morality etc.) if directed towards the attainment of worldly positions such as mentor or teacher of kings (or governments), or towards the acquisition of dignity (titles, degrees), power, retinue, and property, or towards the attainment of rebirth as noble and highly placed humans and *devas*—this is called "Dhamma heritage dependent on the round of rebirths."

There are three forms of the round of rebirth: the round of defilements (*kilesa-vaṭṭa*), the round of *kamma* (*kamma-vaṭṭa*), and the round of *kamma* resultants (*vipākavaṭṭa*). *Vivaṭṭa* means Nibbāna which is the end of these three rounds of rebirths The practice of morality, concentration and wisdom directed towards the ending of these rounds of rebirths is called "Dhamma heritage tending towards the ending of the round of rebirths" (*vivaṭṭa-nissita-dhammadāyajja*).

With reference to the classification of "stable" and "unstable" , the great realm of "proclivity towards personality belief" (*sakkāya diṭṭhi anusaya*) in which worldlings (*puthujjana*) are involved, is like a great and deep ocean of burning hot embers. The morality, concentration and wisdom occasionally practiced by worldlings can be compared to droplets of rain falling into that great ocean of burning hot embers. Such utterances as "I fulfil *sīla*, I possess *sīla*. I practice *samādhi*. I know. I am wise and clever. I perceive mind and matter (*nāma-rūpa*). I contemplate mind and matter" are declarations about morality, concentration and wisdom, which revolve around the personality belief which is concerned with "I" and thus resemble the rain drops falling into the great ocean of red-hot embers. Just as the heat of those embers absorbs the rain drops and makes them disappear, so does the great kingdom of personality belief absorb the worldling's acts of morality, concentration and wisdom and makes them disappear as they are "unstable." Though worldlings may possess morality, concentration and wisdom, their possession of them is temporary (*tadaṅga*).

In the case of *sotāpannas*, their mundane morality of keeping the mundane "precepts with right livelihood as the eighth" (*lokiya-ājivaṭṭhamaka-sīla*); their mundane concentration firmly directed to the noble qualities of the Triple Gem; and their mundane wisdom perceiving the Four Noble Truths—all these are of the rank of stability. They are like rain drops falling into a great lake and never disappear even throughout many lives. This shows the nature of the mundane (*lokiya*) Dhamma heritage.

The supramundane states of morality, concentration and wisdom, the supramundane seventh purification and the requisites of enlightenment (*bodhipakkhiya-dhamma*) accompanying the eight kinds of supramundane consciousness are *vivaṭṭa-nissita* and are stable. Also the mundane morality etc., in the case of *ariyas* who also have attained their supramundane state, are likewise "stable." In such persons, there is no longer any possibility of their becoming *dussīla* (immoral); *asamādhita* (uncomposed), *duppañña* (unwise) or *andhabāla* (foolish).

Persons who lack faith (*saddhā*) and zeal do not even conceive the idea that the higher attainments of the purifications are the heritage which they can acquire in this very life. Because they lack energy (*viriya*), they are reluctant to put forth effort that involves privations. They are liable to reject such effort as impossible. Because they are weak of will, their minds are not fixed on such kind of work. They change their mind whenever they listen to various theories and expositions. Because they lack knowledge and wisdom, they reject such work as being beyond their capabilities.

Therefore the Buddha has urged all beings to strengthen their weak *iddhipādas* (bases of success), such as zeal, etc. Only then can new desires and new thoughts arise.

Only those who possess one or other of the four *iddhipādas* as foundation can enjoy the full benefits of the Buddha's heritage. Others who are without any of these *iddhipādas*, will get the opportunity to enjoy only some of the superficial benefits, without the chance of enjoying the essence of the heritage. Some may not even have the opportunity to enjoy those superficial benefits because they have squandered their heritage and thus become severed from the Buddha's and the Sāsana's heritages.

The heirs of the Sāsana may be classified into: (1) stable or constant heirs; and (2) unstable or inconstant heirs.

People who never obtained knowledge of impermanence and not-self within themselves, are called unstable heirs. They may be disciples or heirs of the Buddha today and may become disciples or heirs of another teacher tomorrow. They may scorn and harm the Buddha Sāsana. Even in the present world there are persons who have changed their faith from the Buddha Sāsana to other religions, and who scorn and undermine the Sāsana. How easily they can change after death and in another birth, can be imagined.

Such a one can be a disciple of the Buddha this month and a disciple of another teacher next month; a disciple of the Buddha this year and the disciple of another teacher next year; a disciple of the Buddha this life and the disciple of another teacher in the next.

Therefore it was said that *puthujjanas* (worldlings) are so called because they look up to the faces of various teachers. This means that, in the unfathomable past *saṃsāra*, worldlings have never been constant in the choice of a teacher in whom they have taken refuge. The occasions on which they have approached a Buddha and taken refuge in him, are very few indeed. Sometimes they took refuge in Brahmā, sometimes in Sakka (Indra), sometimes in various deities, sometimes in planets, spirits and ogres, and they have done so as if these "refuges" were almighty. The number of false teachers is very numerous in the world, and so is the number of existences in which worldlings have taken refuge in such false teachers. While worldlings continue to wander and drift in *saṃsāra*, replete with false attachments to personality belief, they will continue to change their teachers. How frightful, terrible and repellent is the state of a worldling!

Whenever a worldling changes his teacher and refuge, a change also occurs in the doctrines and principles on which he depends for his guidance. Sometimes worldlings accept the purified morality (*adhisīla*) of a Buddha, but more often they accept the moral practices of numerous other teachers. Also, in the matter of views, the existences in which they accept right view are extremely few, while the lives in which they depend on wrong views are extremely numerous. Of the countless errors and perversities possessed by worldlings, that of seeking refuge in false teachers is one of the gravest errors causing them great harm. This is because taking refuge in wrong teachers leads to wrong moral principles and practices, and thus the precious and rare achievement of rebirth as a human being (*manussatta-dullābha*) becomes entirely like a tree producing the evil fruits of rebirth in the worlds of misery, instead of being like a great wishing tree bearing the fruits of good rebirths.

This shows the future path of unstable heirs of the Sāsana.

But those persons who perceive in themselves the characteristics of impermanence (*anicca*) and not-self (*anattā*), are freed from the realm of personality belief. They become stable heirs of the Sāsana. "Stable" means here that throughout their future lives in Samsāra they are no longer inclined to seek refuge in false teachers. They become true children and heirs of the Buddha throughout the future succession of their rebirths. They become members of the "Bon-sin-san" family (see note 64). Their views of the incomparable qualities of the Buddha, the Dhamma and the Sangha become clearer and brighter from one rebirth to another. All the Dhamma heritages will prosper and increase in their minds, i. e. the three path categories (morality etc.), the seven purifications and the thirty-seven requisites of enlightenment. They are beings who will invariably ascend to Anupādisesa-Nibbāna, the extinction of defilements without any groups or existence remaining.

This shows the undeviating path of stable heirs of the Sāsana.

Good and virtuous persons did not put forth effort in past existences which was aimed at their becoming heirs of bad heritages of the Sāsana. They did not practice morality, concentration and wisdom, in order to become heirs of the unstable temporary heritages, but because they wished to become heirs of the stable heritages.

Taking these facts into account, and taking heed of the fact that the Buddha disapproved of the bad heritages of the Sāsana, those persons who have now become disciples of the Buddha should not permit themselves to become bad heirs, nor to become temporary, unstable heirs. They should attempt to become heirs of the good heritages which are the requisites of enlightenment, the *bodhipakkhiya-dhammas*. They should attempt to become stable heirs.

As regards persons deficient in wisdom, the mere performance of good and meritorious acts has to be encouraged as beneficial.

But as to those persons who possess wisdom, if they desire to become stable heirs either in this life or the next, then they should establish in themselves firmly *ājīvaṭṭhamaka sīla* (see note 21.), set up mindful body contemplation and try (for at least three hours a day) to achieve perception of the three characteristics of existence in the five aggregates of "personality." If they perceive any of the three characteristics, they can become "stable" heirs and attain to the status of a "Bon-sin-san"—a stream-enterer.

Here ends the Manual of the Requisites of Enlightenment.

Index

R

S

T

Glossary

(Pali–English and English–Pali

A

Abhikāra: assiduous and successful practice
Absorption, meditative: *jhāna*
Access concentration: *upacāra-samādhi*
Action (volitional): *kamma*
Adhipaññā-sāsana: the teaching of higher wisdom
Adhisīla-sāsana: the teaching of higher morality
Adosa: non-hatred
Aeon: *kappa*
Aggregates: *khandhā*
Ahetuka: one reborn without any good root-conditions
Ājīvaṭṭhamaka-nicca-sīla: permanent practice of morality ending with right livelihood
Akusala: unwholesome, unskillful
Alobha: non-greed
Amata: the Deathless; also refers to great peacefulness or tranquility of mind
Amoha: non-delusion
Anāgami: non-returner
Anamatagga-saṃsāra: the unfathomable aeons of existence
Anattā-bhāvanā: meditation on non-self
Anattā: impersonality, non-self
Anicca: impermanence
Anuppanna: unarisen
Anusaya: proclivity, or latent disposition to the stains
Apāya(-loka): hell, lower world of misery
Āpo: element or liquidity of cohesion (water)
Appanā-samādhi: attainment concentration
Arisen/unarisen: *uppanna/anuppanna.*

Ariya-vaṃsa: the traditional practices of the noble ones.
Ariya: (adj.) noble, holy; (n) noble one, saint
Ascetic observances: *dhutaṅga*
Asubha-bhāvanā: meditation on loathsomeness
Attainnent concentration: *appanā-samādhi*
Attā: Self
Avītikkama : non - transgression
Āyatana: sense bases
Aṭṭhakkhaṇas: (eight) inopportune situations

B

Bāhusacca: great learning
Bala: (four) mental powers
Bhāvanā: (mental) development, i.e., meditation
Bhikkhu, bhikkhunī: Buddhist monk, nun
Bhojane mattaññutā: moderation in eating
bodhipakkhiya-dhamma: requisites of enlightenment
Bodhi: awakening or enlightenment
Bojjhaṅga: (seven) factors of enlightenment
Brahma-vihāra: (four) sublime states; *mettā, karuṇa, mudita,* and *upekkha*
Buddha Sāsana: the dispensation of a Buddha; the time during which a *Sambuddha's* teaching and practice are extant
Buddha, solitary: *Paccekabuddha*

C

Cāga: generosity
Caraṇa: conduct
Chanda, desire, zeal
Characteristics; *lakkhaṇa*
Cittānupassanā: contemplation of the mind
Cittavisuddhi: purification of mind
Citta: consciousness, mind
Compassion: *karuṇā*
Concentration: *samādhi*
Conduct, bad or evil: *duccarita*
Conduct: *caraṇa*
Confidence (faith): *saddhā*
Consciousness: *viññāṇa, citta*
Constant: *nicca*
Constituent groups of existence: *khandā*
Craving, *taṇhā*

D

Dāna: generosity, giving
Dāyaka: one who contributes to a bhikkhu's upkeep
Deathless, the: *amata*
Defilement *kilesa*
Deity: *deva*
Delusion: *moha*
Dependent origination: *paṭicca-samuppāda*
Desire: *chanda*
Deva-loka: divine abode, *deva*-world
Deva: deity, god
Dhammantarāya: danger and obstruction to the Dhamma

Dhammantarāya: obstruction to the Dhamma
Dhammānupassanā: contemplation of mind-objects
Dhamma, danger and obstruction to: *dhammantarāya*
Dhamma: teaching of the Buddha, righteousness, the truth, phenomenon, natural process, duty, righteousness
Dhātu: elements
Dhutaṅga: strict ascetic observances
Dispensation of the Buddha's teaching: *sāsana*
Diṭṭha-dhamma-sukha-vihāra: dwelling at ease in this present existence
Diṭṭhi-visuddhi: purification of view
Diṭṭhi: (wrong) view
Doctine, learning of the: *pariyatti*
Dosa: hate, hatred
Dread (moral): *ottappa*
Duccarita: bad conduct, wrong action
duccarita: evil deeds
Dukkha: suffering
Durājīva: wrong livelihood
Dvi-hetuka: "two root-conditions", i.e., non-greed and non-hate

E

Earth, element of: *paṭhavi*
Effort: *padhāna*
Elements: *dhātu*
Empty: *suñña*
Energy, effort: *viriya* (cf. *paddhāna*)
Enlightenment, requisites of: *bodhipakkhiya-dhamma*
Enlightenment, seven factors of: *bojjhaṅga*
Enlightenment: *bodhi*
Equanimity: *upekkhā*
Evil deeds: *duccarita*

F

Factors of enlightenment (seven): *bojjhaṅga*
Faith: *saddhā*
Fetter: *saṃyojana*
Fruit: *phala*

G

Generosity: *cāga, dāna*
Great primaries: *mahā-bhūtā (paṭhavī, āpo, tejo, vāyo)*
Greed: *lobha*

H

Hair, of the head: *kesā;* of the body: *loma*
Hate, hatred: *dosa*
Heat, fire, element of: *tejo*
Hell: *apāya-loka*
Hiri: moral shame

I

Iddhipāda: base of success
Impermanence: *anicca*
Indriya-saṃvara: guarding the sense-doors
Indriya: faculty
Insight: *vipassanā*
Intention, dedicated: *Pahitatta*

J

Jāgariyānuyoga: wakefulness
Jhānalābhi: attainer of jhānas
Jhāna: absorption, meditative
Joy, altruistic: *muditā*

K

Kāma-loka: world of sensuality
Kamma: (volitional) action
Kammaṭṭhāna: subject of meditation
Kaṅkhāvitaraṇa-visuddhi: purification by overcoming doubt
Kappa: aeon, world-cycle
Karuṇā: compassion
Kāyagatāsati: mindfulness directed to the body
Kāyānupassanā: contemplation of the body
Kesā: hair of the head
Khandhā: constituent groups of existence; aggregates
Kilesa: defilement, stain
Killing a living being: *pāṇātipāta*
Knowledge: *vijjā, ñāṇa*
Kusala: wholesome, skillful

L

Lakkhaṇa: characteristics
Learning, great: *bāhusacca*
Living being: *satta*
Loathsomeness, meditation on: *asubha-bhāvanā*
Lobha: greed
Lokāmisa: worldly rank, honour
Loka: world
Lokuttara: supramundane sphere
Loving kindness: *mettā*

M

Maggāmaggañāṇadassana-visuddhi: purification by knowledge and vision of what is and what is not path
Magga-ñāṇa: path-knowledge
Magga: path
Matter, materiality: *rūpa*
Meditation
subject of: *kammaṭṭhāna*
Meditation device, maṇḍala: *kasiṇa*
Meditative absorption: *jhāna*
Mental obsession: *pariyuṭṭhāna*
Mental phenomena: *nāma*
Merit: *puñña*
Mettā: loving kindness
Micchā: wrong
-dhamma: wrong teachings
Mindfulness of the body: *Kāyagatāsati*
Mindfulness, (four) foundations of: *satipaṭṭhāna*
Mindfulness: *sati*
Mind: *citta*
Moderation in eating: *Bhojane mattaññutā*
Moha: delusion
Monk: *bhikkhu*
Moral dread: *ottappa*
Muditā: altruistic joy

N

Nāma: mind, mentality, mental phenomena (cf. *rūpa*)

Ñāṇadassana-visuddhi : purification by knowledge and vision
Neyya: one who must study and practice in order to attain the paths and fruits
Nibbāna, final: *parinibbāna*
Nicca: constant, permanent (cf. *anicca*
Nimitta: a mental image that may arise during *jhāna*
Nissaya: word for word translation
Niyata-vyākaraṇa: sure prediction
Noble: *ariya*
Non-hatred: *adosa*
Non-returner: *anāgami*
Non-self (impersonality): *anattā*
Non-self, meditation on *anattā-bhāvanā*
Nun: *bhikkhunī*

O

Obstacle: *palibodha*
Ottappa: moral dread

P

Paccekabuddha: solitary Buddha
Padaṭṭhāna: proximate cause
Padhāna: effort
Pahitatta: dedicated intention
Pakati-kusala-kamma: ordinary wholesome acts
Pakati-saddhā: ordinary faith
Palibodha: obstacle
Paññā: wisdom
Pāṇātipāta: killing any living being
Paramattha: ultimate realities
Pāramī: perfection
Parinibbāna: final nibbāna, the passing away of a Buddha
Pariyatti: learning of the doctrine
Pariyuṭṭhāna: mental obsession,
Path-knowledge: *magga-ñāṇa*
Path: *magga*
Paṭhavi: element of extension (earth)
Paṭiccasamuppāda: dependent origination
Paṭipadāñāṇadassana-visuddhi: purification by knowledge and vision of the way
Perfection: *pārami*
Personality-belief: *sakkāya-diṭṭhi*
Person: *puggala*
Phala: fruit, fruition
Pleasure: *sukha*
Powers, (four) mental: *bala*
Practice, assiduous and successful: *abhikāra*
Prediction, sure: *niyata vyākaraṇa*
Proclivity (a dominant mental state): *anusaya*
Proximate cause: *padaṭṭhāna*
Puggala: person
Puññantarāya: obstruction to the performance of meritorious actions
Puñña: merit
Pure abodes: *Suddhāvāsa-brahma-loka*

Purification: *visuddhi*

R

Rains, rains-retreat: *vassa*
Realities, ultimate: *paramattha*
Rebirth, cycle of: *saṃsāra*
Recollection of the past: *vāsanā*
Requisite ingredient: *sambhāra*
Requisites of enlightenment: *Bodhipakkhiya-dhamma*
Right exertion or effort *sammāpadhāna*
Right thought: *sammā-saṇkappa*
Right understanding, views: *sammā-diṭṭhi*
Rūpa: matter, materiality

S

Sacca; truth
Saddhamma: the seven attributes of good and virtuous people—*saddhā, sati, hiri, ottappa, bāhusacca, viriya, & paññā*
Saddhā: faith, confidence
Saṃsāra: the cycle or round of rebirths
Saṃyojana: fetter
Sakkāya-diṭṭhi: personality-belief
Samādhi: concentration
Samatha-manasikāra-citta-visuddhi: the practice of purification of mind consisting of advertence of mind to tranquillity
Samatha-vipassanā-manasikāra: advertence of mind towards tranquility and insight
Samatha: tranquility
Sambhāra: requisite ingredient, material
Sammā-diṭṭhi: right understanding, views
Sammāpaddhāna: right exertion or effort
Sammasana-ñāṇa: Exploring, contemplating, or knowing all phenomena of existence as impermanent, suffering, and non-self
Sammā-saṅkappa: right thought
Sāsana: dispensation of the Buddha's teaching
Satipaṭṭhāna: (four) foundations of mindfulness
Sati: mindfulness
Satta: living being
Self : *attā*
Sense base: *āyatana*
Shame: *hiri*
Sikkhā: training
Sīla-visuddhi: purification of virtue
Sīla: morality (not killing, stealing, etc.)
Skillful (wholesome): *kusala*
Sotāpattimagga: path of stream-entry
Sublime states (the four): *brahma-vihaāra*
Suddhāvāsa-brahma-loka: the heavenly realms known as "pure abodes"
Suffering: *dukkha*
Sufficient condition: *upanissaya*
Sukha: pleasure
Sukkhavipassaka: one who practices *vipassanā* only

Suñña: empty, void
Supramundane sphere: *lokuttara*

T

Taṇhā: craving
Tejo: heat, element of
Thought, initial: *vitakka;* sustained: *vicāra*
Tihetuka: one reborn with three good root-conditions
Tiratana: triple gem
Training: *sikkhā*
Tranquillity: *samatha*
Transgression: *vītikama*
Triple gem: *tiratana*
Truth: *sacca*

U

Ugghātiṭaññū: one who understands immediately
Unarisen: *anuppanna*
Unwholesome (unskillful): *akusala*
Upacāra-samādhi: access concentration
Upanissaya: sufficient condition
Upāsakā, (upāsika): lay male (female) disciples
Upekkhā: equanimity
Uposatha-sīla: precepts observed on Uposatha days
Uppanna/anuppanna: arisen/ unarisen

V

Vāsanā: recollection of the past; accumulation of good habits & potentials
Vassa: rains, rainy seasons (a time of retreat when monks traditionally remain in one temple)
Vāyo: element of wind or motion
Vedanānupassanā: contemplation of feelings
Views (or wrong view), *diṭṭhi,* or *(micca-diṭṭhī)*
Vijjā-caraṇa: knowledge-and-conduct
Vijjā: knowledge, science
Viññāṇa: consciousness
Vipañcitaññū: one who attains the paths and fruits after hearing a long discourse
Vipassanā insight
Viriya: energy, effort, diligence
Visuddhi: purification
Vitakka: thought-conception, "initial thought"
Vītikama: transgression (in deeds or speech)

W

Water, element of: *āpo*
Wholesome: *kusala*
Wind or motion, element of: *vāyo*
Wisdom: *paññā*
World: *loka*
Wrong: *micchā;* cf. *sammā*
w. livelihood: *micchā-ājīva*
w. teachings: *micchā dhammā*

Z

Zeal: *chanda*

ABOUT PARIYATTI

Pariyatti is dedicated to providing affordable access to authentic teachings of the Buddha about the Dhamma theory (*pariyatti*) and practice (*paṭipatti*) of Vipassana meditation. A 501(c)(3) non-profit charitable organization since 2002, Pariyatti is sustained by contributions from individuals who appreciate and want to share the incalculable value of the Dhamma teachings. We invite you to visit www.pariyatti.org to learn about our programs, services, and ways to support publishing and other undertakings.

Pariyatti Publishing Imprints

Vipassana Research Publications (focus on Vipassana as taught by S.N. Goenka in the tradition of Sayagyi U Ba Khin)

BPS Pariyatti Editions (selected titles from the Buddhist Publication Society, co-published by Pariyatti in the Americas)

Pariyatti Digital Editions (audio and video titles, including discourses)

Pariyatti Press (classic titles returned to print and inspirational writing by contemporary authors)

Pariyatti enriches the world by

- disseminating the words of the Buddha,
- providing sustenance for the seeker's journey,
- illuminating the meditator's path.